ANTHOLOGY OF KUMĀRILABHAṬṬA'S WORKS

ANTHOLOGY

OF

KUMĀRILABHAṬṬA'S WORKS

WITH PREFACE AND INTRODUCTION

PERI SARVESWARA SHARMA

FOREWORD BY

PROF. WILHELM RAU

MOTILAL BANARSIDASS

Delhi :: Varanasi :: Patna

1st Edition : Delhi, 1980

ISBN: 978-81-2082-084-5

Also available at:

MOTILAL BANARSIDASS
41 U.A. Bungalow Road, Jawahar Nagar, Delhi 110 007
8 Mahalaxmi Chamber, Warden Road, Mumbai 400 026
120 Royapettah High Road, Mylapore, Chennai 600 004
Sanas Plaza, Subhash Nagar, Pune 411 002
16 St. Mark's Road, Bangalore 560 001
8 Camac Street, Calcutta 700 017
Ashok Rajpath, Patna 800 004
Chowk, Varanasi 221 0011

PRINTED IN INDIA
BY JAINENDRA PRAKASH JAIN AT SHRI JAINENDRA PRESS,
A-45 NARAINA, PHASE I, NEW DELHI 110 028
AND PUBLISHED BY NARENDRA PRAKASH JAIN FOR
MOTILAL BANARSIDASS PUBLISHERS PRIVATE LIMITED,
BUNGALOW ROAD, DELHI 110 007

DEDICATED TO MY FATHER

Peri Veṅkaṭeśa Śāstrī

FOREWORD

Kumārilabhaṭṭa's commentary on Śabarasvāmin's Bhāṣya on Jaimini's Pūrvamīmāṃsāsūtra has been printed in its entirety only once in Banaras (Mīmāṃsāślokavārttika with Pārthasārathi Miśra's Nyāyaratnākara, 1898-99; Mīmāṃsātantravārttika, 1882-1903; Ṭupṭīkā, 1903-04), and a reliable English translation was prepared by Sir Ganganatha Jha of the Ślokavārttika (Calcutta 1900-08) as well as of the Tantravārttika (Calcutta 1903-24). A Trivandrum edition of the Ślokavārttika with Sucaritamiśra's Kāśikā has, unfortunately, until now remained unfinished (Part I: 1927, Part II: 1929, Part III : 1943 up to the Sambandhākṣepavārttika of the Autpattikasūtra).

All of these books have been out of print for decades and nowadays are hardly available anywhere except in a few Public Libraries. Convinced that Kumārilabhaṭṭa was a master-mind of the first order and finding his sayings quoted very often by other philosophers, although invariably without exact reference, Dr. P.S. Sharma has, after a diligent and prolonged study, prepared an anthology of the more important kārikās in alphabetical arrangement, to make up for the want of a complete edition. It is hoped that this collection will be welcome to students of Indian Philosophy, as it may serve not only as an appetizer and an introduction to tenets of Pūrvamīmāṃsā but also as a means to trace anonymous quotations in other texts of kindred nature.

Marburg an der Lahn Wilhelm Rau

CONTENTS

PREFACE

This work contains two hundred and twenty-four *kārikās* from the *Ślokavārttika*, and one hundred and ninety four *kārikās* from the *Tantravārttika* of Kumārila Bhaṭṭa. This selection from Kumārila Bhaṭṭa's works represents his views on different topics of the (*Pūrva-*)*Mīmāṃsāśāstra.* Many of these selected *kārikās* have often been cited by authors belonging to different schools of philosophy. In my present work, the selected *kārikās* have been arranged in alphabetical order. With the help of this work, one can easily find out the sources of *kārikās*. One can also have, with the help of the present selection, a complete knowledge of views of the Mīmāṃsakas on important subjects such as, Creation and Dissolution of the world; the nature of *Ātman*; the nature of *Dharma*; the Highest Good; the *Svarga*; the nature of *Śabda*; Self-Validity of the *Veda*; *Sphoṭa* theory; Generality; Individuality; Negation; *Śūnyavāda*; *Vijñānavāda*; *Apohavāda*; the Creator; the theory of *Apūrva*; the Omniscient; etc. etc. The only condition is that the reader must have a little knowledge of the Sanskrit language. However, in order to encourage the study of this work, I would like to give translation of a few *kārikās* on varied topics:

On *Dharmajijñāsā* :

jijñāsyaḥ saṃśayād dharmaḥ śreyaskaratayāpi ca,
asaṃdigdho hy ajijñāsyo yo vā syān niṣprayojanaḥ.
(p. 40)

Dharma must be investigated on account of the

doubt (that arises with regard to the true meaning of Dharma) and because it (i.e. Dharma) brings about the highest good, while (an object—artha) which is neither doubtful nor useful need not be investigated.

Difference between the *Yogācāra* and *Mādhyamika* :

tatrārthaśūnyaṃ vijñānaṃ yogācāraḥ samāśritaḥ,
tasyāpy abhāvam icchanti ye mādhyamikavādinaḥ.
(p. 41)

In this connection the *Yogācāra* (-philosopher) assumes that consciousness is devoid of (real) objects. Those who profess the *Mādhyamika* (philosophy) maintain that even this (i.e. consciousness) does not exist, really.

Attacking the *Vijñānavāda* :

ekaṃ ced grāhakaṃ grāhyaṃ kuto bhinnatvavāg iyam
bhinnaṃ cet katham ucyeta tasyaikatvaṃ punas tvayā.
(p. 38)

If the consciousness and the object of the consciousness are identical (lit. if the receiver and the received are identical), how can you speak of them differently (lit. wherefrom this speech of difference) ? And if (they are) different, how can you, on the other hand, postulate (their) identity ?

On the Svarga :

uptamātre na hi vrīhau phalam utpadyate kva cit,
athāṅkuro 'pi tatra syāt svargo 'py astīti gamyatām.
(p. 38)

For crop does nowhere appear immediately upon the sowing of rice-grains,—a sprout (i.e. a slow development) must be (assumed) in this connection, too. It may be understood that there *is* also a heavenly existence.

On the nature of the soul (*Ātman, Puṃs, Nara*) :

śarīrendriyabuddhibhyo vyatiriktatvam ātmanaḥ,
nityatvaṃ ceṣyate śeṣaṃ śarīrādi vinaśyati.
(p. 52)

It is desired that the Ātman be different from the body, the sense-organs, and the intellect, and that it be eternal. The rest (i.e.) the body etc. is destroyed.

sukhaduḥkhādyavasthāś ca gacchann api naro mama,
caitanyadravyasattvādirūpaṃ naiva vimuñcati.
(p. 54)

Although the soul experiences (lit. moves into different) states (like) happiness, sorrow, etc., yet—in my opinion—he never forgoes his form, namely consciousness, substantiality, existence, etc.

jñānaśaktisvabhāvo 'to nityaḥ sarvagataḥ pumān,
dehāntarakṣamaḥ kalpyaḥ so 'gacchann eva yokṣyate.
(p. 41)

Hence, the eternal, all-pervasive soul, possessing the power of knowledge, should be taken as capable of (assuming) another body. Not moving, he will yet be yoked (to another body, after death).

Attacking the *Apohavāda* of Buddhists :

vastvantarasya cābhāvāt tasyāpoho 'pi duṣkaraḥ,
nājñānaṃ nāma kiṃ cit syād apohyaṃ jñānavādinām.
(p. 51)

For those who uphold the doctrine that only consciousness is real and its objects are not real (*jñānavādin*), since there is no other object existing, its exclusion is also difficult. (For *jñānavādins*, the object) to be excluded would not be something different from consciousness.

On ultimate reality of phonemes :

yāvanto yādṛśā ye ca yadarthapratipādane,
varṇāḥ prajñātasāmarthyās te tathaivāvabodhakāḥ.
(p. 50)

The very phonemes, which by their number and qualities are known as capable to denote a certain meaning, also serve to communicate the idea.

Refuting the *Sphoṭa* theory of the grammarians :

varṇā vā dhvanayo vāpi sphoṭam na padavākyayoḥ,
vyañjanti vyañjakatvena yathā dīpaprabhādayaḥ.
(p. 50)

Neither the phonemes (*varṇa*) nor the sounds (*dhvani*) can manifest the *sphoṭa* of either a word or a sentence in the way a lamp or sunlight etc. (do manifest themselves as well as an object) due to their capability of manifesting.

nārthasya vācakaḥ sphoṭo varṇebhyo vyatirekataḥ,
ghaṭādivan na dṛṣṭena virodho dharmasiddhitaḥ.
(p. 45)

(There is nothing (like) *sphoṭa* different from phonemes (which is) expressive of meaning. (There is) no clash with what is seen in the case of a pot because capacity (of phonemes in expressing meaning) has been established. (It means the example of light and pot is not possible here.)

Buddhists do not accept Generality (*jāti*). But they assume that when we utter the word *gauḥ* (cow), each and every individual of cow is understood because they are all similar to each other (*sadṛśa*) or because they do possess equal form (*sarūpa*). Refuting this view :

tena sārūpyaśabdena kiṃ punaḥ pratipadyate,
samānarūpabhāvaś cej jātiḥ sāsmābhir iṣyate.
(p. 43)

What, after all, is achieved with this term *sārūpya*? If it means the existence of objects possessing a similar form, then we call this (simply) *jāti*.

sādṛśyam atha sārūpyaṃ kasya keneti kathyatām,
na tāvac chābaleyena bāhuleyādayaḥ samāḥ.
(p. 54)

Pray, the similarity (and) further the equal form of whom (or : of which) with whom (or : with which) (do you mean) ? The offsprings of *Bahulā* (a black cow ?) etc. are by no means equal to the offspring of *Śabalā* (a spotted cow).

On the Creation and Dissolution of the world :

yadā sarvam idaṃ nāsīt kvāvasthā tatra gamyatām,
prajāpateḥ kva vā sthānaṃ kiṃrūpaṃ ca pratīyatām.
(p. 49)

When (in the beginning) this all was non-existent, how (lit. where) could the state (of things) be understood ? Where was the seat of the Creator (*Prajāpati*) and in which form was it ?

pravṛttiḥ katham ādyā ca jagataḥ saṃpratīyate,
śarīrāder vinā cāsya katham icchāpi sarjane.
(p. 47)

How is the primordial origin of the world to be

understood? How could he (i.e. *Prajāpati*), without (possessing) the body etc., have even desire to create (the world)?

sādhanaṃ cāsya dharmādi tadā kiṃ cin na vidyate,
na ca niḥsādhanaḥ kartā kaś cit sṛjati kiṃcana.
(p. 54)

Moreover, at that time there is no instrument for creation as Dharma etc. at his disposal. No agent, however, could create anything when he lacked the (necessary) instrument.

tathā cāpekṣamāṇasya svātantryaṃ pratihanyate,
jagac cāsṛjatas tasya kiṃ nāmeṣṭam na sidhyati.
(p. 42)

And the independence of (*Prajāpati*) thus depending (on some instrument for creation) is contradicted. Besides, which desire of his would remain unfulfilled if he did not create the world?

krīḍārthāyāṃ pravṛttau ca vihanyeta kṛtārthatā,
bahuvyāpāratāyāṃ ca kleśo bahutaro bhavet.
(p. 39)

And if the creation (of the world) were but for (*Prajāpati's*) amusement, purposefulness (of the creation) would be denied. Moreover, because it (i.e. the creation of the world) requires much effort, the nuisance would be greater (for *Prajāpati* than the enjoyment).

pralaye 'pi pramāṇaṃ naḥ sarvacchedātmake na hi,
na ca prayojanaṃ tena syāt prajāpatikarmaṇā.
(p. 47)

For, with regard to the complete dissolution (of the world) also, we have no authoritative statement. And by this action of *Prajāpati*, no purpose would be served with.

iśvarecchā yadīṣyeta saiva syāl lokakāraṇam,
īśvarecchāvaśitve hi niṣphalā karmakalpanā.
(p. 37)

If the will of God were to be postulated (as the reason for the dissolution of the world), the same would be the reason for (his) creating the world. If (all) were dependent on the will of God, the performance of religious actions would, after all, be useless.

tasmān na paramāṇvāder ārambhaḥ syāt tadicchayā,
puruṣasya ca śuddhasya nāśuddhā vikṛtir bhavet.
(p. 43)

Hence, creation (of the world) from the infinitesimal particle of an atom etc. could not take place through his (i.e. God's) will. And (the theory that the world might be the transformation of the pure *Puruṣa* is also false, because) no transformation of the pure *Puruṣa* could ever be impure.

svayaṃ ca śuddharūpatvād asattvāc cānyavastunaḥ,
svapnādivad avidyāyāḥ pravṛttis tasya kiṃkṛtā.
(p. 55)

And if, because he himself is of pure form and because no other thing exists, (the creation) is but an illusion (*avidyā*) like a dream; what causes the origin (of *avidyā*) in him (i.e. in the pure *Puruṣa*) ?

mithyājñānaṃ na tatrāsti rāgadveṣādayo 'pi vā,
manovṛttir hi sarveṣāṃ na cotpannaṃ tadā manaḥ.
(p. 48)

(Before the creation), there is neither false knowledge nor love nor hate etc. For a mental operation (is the cause) for them all, and at that time (i.e. at the time of the creation) the mind is not (yet) existent.

sargapralayavijñānaṃ samastajagadāśrayam,
svaśarīravidāṃ puṃsāṃ nādhikyenopayujyate.
(p. 53)

Knowledge concerning the creation and the dissolution of the world as a whole is not particularly useful to men who are conscious of their own body (i.e. who realize that they are mortal).

On the Creator :

sarvajñavan niṣedhyā ca sraṣṭuḥ sadbhāvakalpanā,
na ca dharmād ṛte tasya bhavel lokād viśiṣṭatā.
(p. 53)

The idea of the real existence of a creator ought to be abandoned just as (the idea of the real existence) of an omniscient (man). Besides, without *Dharma*, he (i.e. the creator) would not be superior to people.

Philipps-Universität, Peri Sarveswara Sharma
Marburg/Lahn.

INTRODUCTION

Kumārila Bhaṭṭa is a unique figure in the history of the *Mīmāṃsāśāstra*. Because of his reformatory views, his works have created a new School. This school is called *Bhāṭṭa*. This *Bhāṭṭa* school has become more popular than that of *Prābhākara* which has stuck to the orthodox view. The *Bhāṭṭa* school has won many followers like Maṇḍana Miśra, Pārthasārathi Miśra, etc. In comparison with the *Prābhākara* school the *Bhāṭṭa* school has widely been studied in India.

Kumārila Bhaṭṭa has composed three works, namely : *Ślokavārttika*, *Tantravārttika*, and *Ṭupṭīkā*. The *Ślokavārttika* is a commentary in verses (*kārikās*) on the first *pāda* of the first *adhyāya* (chapter) of Śabarasvāmin's *Bhāṣya* on Jaimini's *Mīmāṃsā-sūtras*. The first *pāda* of the first *adhyāya* is otherwise known as the *tarkapāda*. The *Tantravārttika* is a commentary in the mixture of prose and verses beginning from the 2nd *pāda* of the first *adhyāya* to the end of the third *adhyāya*. The *Ṭupṭīkā* is a scanty commentary on the remaining nine *adhyāyas* of Śabarasvāmin's *Bhāṣya* on the *Sūtras* of Jaimini. These three works together form a complete commentary on the *Mīmāṃsābhāṣya*.

In the end of his introductory kārikās to the *Ślokavārttika*, Kumārila Bhaṭṭa gives the reason for composing his commentary on the *Mīmāṃsābhāṣya* as follows :

prāyeṇaiva hi mīmāṃsā loke lokāyatīkṛtā,
tām āstikapathe kartum ayaṃ yatnaḥ kṛto mayā.
(p. 47)

> This effort has been made by me to bring the *Mīmāṃsāśāstra* on the track of those who believe in the authority of the *Veda*; because this *Śāstra* has almost been reduced to the level of *Cārvākadarśana* (eat, drink and enjoy-philosophy).

This introductory kārikā indicates a chaotic condition of the *Mīmāṃsāśāstra* at the time of Kumārila Bhaṭṭa. This chaotic condition had arisen not only from an outside attack—namely by the Cārvākas, Bauddhas, Jainas etc.—on the theories of the Mīmāṃsakas, but also from an inside attack, i.e. the attack that came from within the *āstika* community, which had used to give importance to the *Upaniṣads* and mystic portion of the *Veda* neglecting the ritual portion. This trend has already been evidenced in the *Bhagavadgītā* wherein the *Mīmāṃsā* representing the ritual portion has been reduced to a lower level :

yām imāṃ puṣpitāṃ vācam pravadanty avipaścitaḥ,
vedavādaratāḥ pārtha nānyad astīti vādinaḥ.

kāmātmānaḥ svargaparā janmakarmaphalapradām,
kriyāviśeṣabahulāṃ bhogaiśvaryagatiṃ prati.

bhogaiśvaryaprasaktānāṃ tayāpahṛtacetasām,
vyavasāyātmikā buddhiḥ samādhau na vidhīyate.
(2.42-44)

> O Arjuna, those who are obsessed by desire and devoted to the letter of the *Vedas*, who look upon heaven as the supreme goal and argue that there is nothing beyond heaven, are unwise. They utter flowery speech recommending many acts of various kinds for the attainment of pleasure and prosperity with rebirth as their fruit. Those whose minds are carried away by such words, and who

are deeply attached to pleasure and worldly prosperity, cannot attain the determinate intellect in the *samādhi* (=concentration).

Kumārila Bhaṭṭa

It is not known to us definitely, when and in which part of India Kumārila Bhāṭṭa was born and lived. But it is certain that he lived after the grammarian Bhartṛhari and the Buddhist Diṅnāga and before Maṇḍana Miśra. Probably he is a contemporary of Dharmakīrti, a Buddhist philosopher and the author of the *Pramāṇavārttika*. However, I would like to reproduce here the account given by different scholars about Kumārila Bhaṭṭa.

S. Radhakrishnan writes :

> Kumārila,[1] the vigorous exponent of Brahmanical orthodoxy which assumes the authoritativeness of the Vedas and the supremacy of the priest, commented on the *Sūtra* and the *Bhāṣya*, and his work is in three parts. The first *Ślokavārttika* deals with the first part of the first chapter. The second *Tantravārttika* takes us to the end of Chapter III, and *Ṭupṭīkā* covers the rest. Kumārila is earlier than Śaṁkara, and may be assigned to the seventh century A.D.[2]

1. Kumārila, reputed to be a great champion of Hinduism, is said to be a Brahmin of Bihar converted from Buddhism to Hinduism. See Eliot : *Hinduism and Buddhism*, vol. ii, pp. 110, 207. Tāranātha makes him a native of South India. According to the tradition, Kumārila wanted to commit himself to the flames for two sins, which are the destruction of his Buddhist *guru* and the practical denial of God in his anxiety to prove the eternal character of the Vedas and the exclusive efficiency of Vedic ceremonialism to salvation. See Mādhava's *Śaṁkaradigvijaya*.

2. According to Mr. Paṇḍit, Kumārila was the *guru* of Bhavabhūti (A.D. 620-680), and so is assigned to A.D. 590-650. This agrees with the admitted fact that the fame of Kumārila was well established in the later days of Harṣa.

Prabhākara[1] wrote his commentary *Bṛhatī* on the *Bhāṣya* of Śabara, which it closely follows. Kumārila rejects now and then Śabara's views. From the fact that Prabhākara does not take notice of Kumārila's views, while Kumārila refers to views similar to those set forth in the *Bṛhatī*,[2] it is sometimes urged that Prabhākara preceded Kumārila. The style of *Bṛhatī* is said to indicate its earlier date.[3*]

Paṇḍit Gopīnath Kaviraj gives the following information about Kumārila Bhaṭṭa :

Kumārila's place in Indian Thought

The time does not seem to have yet arrived when we can correctly assign to Kumārila his proper place in the history of contemporary Indian thought. But it is certain that he was, like his successor Śaṅkarācārya, the foremost protagonist of Vedic revival. The early Hindu revival which

1. According to the tradition, Prabhākara and Maṇḍana were the pupils of Kumārila, who gave Prabhākara the title of "guru" in recognition of his brilliant powers.

2. i.2.31; i.3.2; i.4.1.

3. Jhā : *Prabhākara School*; Keith : *Karma Mīmāṃsā*. Professor Kuppuswāmi Śāstri supports the traditional view, and argues at some length against the position taken up by Jhā and Keith. See his paper on *The Prabhākara School of Pūrva Mīmāṃsā, Proceedings of the Second Oriental Conference*, Calcutta. An old South Indian tradition states that Uṁveka was a pupil of Kumārila.

Uṁvekaḥ kārikāṁ vetti, campūṁ vetti prabhākaraḥ,
Maṇḍanas tūbhayaṁ vetti nobhayaṁ vetti revaṇaḥ.

Mr. Paṇḍit, in his Introduction to *Gauḍavaho* (Bombay Skt. Series) quotes the verse with the words Tantra and Vāmana in the places of Campū and Maṇḍana. See also Guṇaratna's *Ṣaḍdarśanasamuccaya Vṛtti* (1409). Uṁveka is identified with Bhavabhūti and regarded as one of the pupils of Kumārila. See also Citsukha's *Advaita Pradīpikā*, p. 265.

* S. Radhakrishnan : *Indian Philosophy*, Vol. II, reprinted 1951. New York : The Macmillan Company, London : George Allen & Unwin Ltd. pp. 377-378.

took place in the days of the Śuṅgas and Kāṇvas was characterised by an eager desire to re-establish the glory of the Vedic rituals. As it was Karma-Kāṇḍa against which the early Buddhism carried on its crusade, it was the same which raised its head when the dominant hand of the last great Maurya Emperor was laid low in death. The performance of Aśvamedha was only a symbolical event. The same thing recurred under the Guptas, after Buddhism had once more emerged in the days of Kaniṣka and his immediate successors. But there was this difference, viz. that though Hinduism reappeared in a new form, Buddhism was not still on its way to decline. Far from it. The Gupta and Harsha periods form really, from the strictly intellectual standpoint, the most brilliant epoch in the development of Indian Philosophy. The two religions flourished side by side. The accounts of Fa Hien, Hiouen Tsang and Itsing furnish no evidence of mutual animosity or bitterness or struggle of one party to gain ascendance over the other. But the most remarkable feature of the age was that apart from Śaiva, Vaiṣṇava and Tāntrika renaissance, of which no reasonable doubt exists, there appeared a re-awakening of interest in the complexity of Vedic ritualism. The composition of a work like the Tantra-Vārttika would be an anomaly—nay, an absurdity—in an age in which, by reason of absence of ritualistic practices, the technical details so elaborately set forth in the work would lose their significance.

It is interesting to observe that this is exactly the period when Buddhism began to decline. And it is generally believed that Kumārila, the protagonist of Vedic ritualism, was one of the most potent forces actively employed in bringing about this decline.

Kumārila and Buddhism

There were many internal causes which led to the disintegration of Buddhist Church. The corruption of the Church was one such factor. The abuse of Tantric practices ended in moral degeneration; and there was an absolute lack of any element of check or restraint upon the free play of the passions. All this tended to the overthrow of the dignity of Buddhism.

The story of persecution is however exaggerated. Even assuming that the Buddhists were persecuted by Mihir Gula and the Hunas in Kashmir, by Śaśāṅka Narendra, and by others, these are hardly worth mention, being so few and far between. The belief that Kumārila instigated Sudhanvan to root out Buddhism at the point of the sword is not historically correct,[1] though Kumārila's tirades against the Buddhists are numerous, and in many cases they are well founded. In the *Śaṅkara Digvijaya* of Mādhava (7.90) Kumārila is reported to have said that the Buddhist teachers with their own following used to propitiate kings and through them to persuade people to accept Buddhism and discard Vedic faith. This sort of invidious procedure was certainly such as was likely to bring down contempt upon its followers,

1. It is not believed by historians; cf. Eliot, Radhakrishnan, Carpenter, etc. The struggle between Buddhism and Hinduism was a war of the pen and not of the sword.

and it actually set aflame an independent spirit like that of Kumārila with righteous indignation. The statement of the *Digvijaya* (7.90) is not unworthy of credence, for we know that Buddhism had always been a religion of royal patronage. It had no stamina to grow from within under its own auspices. Aśoka, Kaniṣka and others extended patronage towards it and gave it a push forward, on which it became popular and universal; but as soon as such patronage and the missionary activities which it implied were withdrawn it shrank back within narrow limits and its progress was at once arrested. The entire history of this faith bears a similar nature.

In Kumārila's time the Buddhist University of Nālandā was still in flourishing condition, and there was a large number of Buddhist thinkers all over the country. Hindu philosophical thought was mercilessly attacked in all quarters. In Nyāya Uddyotakara who had already recovered his Science, especially Vātsyāyana's work, from the attack of Dignāga, was himself made the victim of bitter assaults. Probably Dharmakīrti was one of these assailants. It was left to Vācaspati in a subsequent century to reclaim Uddyotakara. The Vedic culture was also eclipsed by the Buddhists. And we find in Kumārila's Vārttikas, more particularly in the Śloka-Vārttika, a vehement criticism of the Buddhist philosophy. To one who has carefully studied the Tantra-Vārttika and the Śloka-Vārttika, it will be evident that Kumārila was very fully acquainted with the various Buddhist systems.

Kumārila's Conversion

There is a tradition recorded in Tibetan works, e.g. Chos-byun by Tāranātha and Dpag-bsam-ljon-bzan (ed. by Sarat Chandra Das), that there was a controversy between Kumārila Bhaṭṭa and the Buddhist philosopher Dharmakīrti. It is said that Dharmakīrti, desiring acquaintance with the secrets of the Hindu Philosophy and hearing that Kumārila Bhaṭṭa was the greatest exponent of the Tīrthika system, disguised himself as a slave and entered into Kumārila's service. Satisfied with his work Kumārila expounded to him the secret doctrines. Thereupon Dharmakīrti left off his employment and invited all Brahmanic philosophers to an open controversy with him. It is said that the debate lasted several months, and that many Brahmans who were defeated were converted to Buddhism. Kumārila, with a large following, then entered the lists. It was arranged that whoever was defeated should adopt the doctrines of the winner. The debate took place and Kumārila with his followers was defeated and converted to Buddhism.[1]

In the *Śaṅkara Digvijaya* of Mādhava we find however a different account. Reading the two accounts together we feel convinced that Dharmakīrti in disguise studied with Kumārila who gave out his secrets to him in confidence. But Kumārila was not then as fully conversant with Buddhist Philosophy as Dharmakīrti had become with Hinduism, and the result was that Kumārila was defeated in debate. This defeat of Kumārila

1. S. C. Vidyābhūṣaṇa, *History of Indian Logic* (1923), pp. 304-5.

is recorded in the Tibetan tradition and is supported by the evidence of Mādhava :

avādiṣaṃ vedavighātadakṣais
tannāśakaṃ jetum abudhyamānaḥ,
tadīyasiddhāntarahasyavārdhīn
niṣedhyabodhād dhi niṣedhyabādhaḥ.

Kumārila confesses here plainly that being ignorant of the secrets of the Buddhist Thought he was not able to defeat his Buddhist opponents in debate. Tradition also has it that Kumārila, by birth a Brāhmaṇa, had been a Buddhist monk but that he abjured it and adopted Hinduism (Eliot, *Hinduism and Buddhism*, II, pp.110.207). It is said that Kumārila wept once on hearing the Veda refuted. The Buddhists suspected him, seeing the tears. They threw him down from the roof of a high building, on which Kumārila exclaimed : "If Śrutis, are authoritative then I shall live." For the hesitant expression (viz. "if") and for hearing Śāstras, in disguise (vyājena), one eye of Kumārila was destroyed. Kumārila says that the teacher of a single letter is to be worshipped as a Guru, while his teacher was omniscient (*sarvajña*) and yet he denied him—an unpardonable fault.

Kumārila's Last Scene

We owe it to the *Śaṅkara Digvijaya* that Kumārila committed suicide by entering the flames in order to expiate (*apākariṣṇuḥ*) his sins. He says that his sins were twofold, viz. (1) that, though he accepted discipleship under a Buddhist teacher he set himself subsequently against him and his doctrines. This was an unpardonable sin (*guror unmathanaprasaktaṃ mahattaraṃ doṣam apākariṣṇuḥ*). (2) The other fault consisted in denial of the Godhead.

It is said that Śaṅkara, who had already prepared his Bhāṣyas, met Kumārila on his death-bed on the pyre, when his body was already half-burnt. Śaṅkara asked Kumārila to prepare a Vārttika on his Bhāṣya and on Kumārila's refusal to comply with his request on the ground of there being no time for it, he offered to revive him by means of his Supreme Yogic power, if the latter only consented to it. But Kumārila did not like the idea.

Contrast with Śaṅkara re *Buddhism* :

It is a well-known fact that both Kumārila and Śaṅkara comprise in themselves the best intellectual fruits of the anti-Buddhist reaction which was already set afoot in the Gupta revival of the earlier centuries. In this respect both of them occupy a footing of equality. But from a careful comparison of the contents of Śaṅkara's Bhāṣyas and of Kumārila's Vārttikas the conclusion seems irresistible that Kumārila's knowledge of Buddhist Philosophy was more profound and more accurate, though Śaṅkara is better known as having been more deeply influenced by Buddhism. The nickname *pracchannabauddha*, which was applied to Śaṅkara by the Vaiṣṇavas (and by Vijñāna Bhikṣu) and in certain Purāṇas, was not unfounded. But it seems, as Prof. Yamakami has brilliantly shown in his *Systems of Buddhist Thought* that Śaṅkara's knowledge of Buddhist Philosophy was naturally superficial, inasmuch as he had no access to the secrets of its teachings.

Kumārila's Native Place

There are no certain data for determining the birth-place of Bhaṭṭa Kumārila. Tāranātha says that he was a native of Southern India. But it is also believed that he was a Brahman of Bihar who abjured Buddhism for Hinduism.[1] The tradition associating Kumārila with Northern India receives some support from the statement of Ānandagiri in his *Śaṅkara Vijaya* (Calcutta Edition, p.235) that Kumārila came from the North (udagdeśāt[2]) and persecuted the Buddhists and Jains in the South.

Kumārila's Family Life

We know nothing about Kumārila's family life. The Tibetan works assert that Kumārila was a family man. He was in possession of a large number of rice fields and 500 male and 500 female slaves, and he was liberally patronised by his king. Ānandagiri's statement[3] that Maṇḍana was Kumārila's sister's husband (*bhaginībhartā*) is not probably correct. Mādhavācārya however observes that Maṇḍana was Kumārila's pupil.

Kumārila's Religious Belief

It is hardly possible to make a definite pronouncement on the religious convictions of Kumārila. Whatever the position of Pūrva Mīmāṃsā might have been in this respect, Kumārila was

1. Eliot, Sir Charles, *Hinduism and Buddhism*, Vol. II, pp. 110, 207.

2. The term *udagdeśa* is vague. It may loosely stand for any part of Northern India from Kashmir to Magadha and Bengal, though generally the term is used for Kashmir and the Punjab. Magadha and Bengal are usually reckoned among the eastern countries.

3. *Śaṅkara Vijaya* (Bib. Ind. Edn., pp. 236-37).

very probably not an atheist in the ordinary sense of the term. The introductory verse of the *Śloka-Vārttika* runs thus :

viśuddhajñānadehāya trivedīdivyacakṣuṣe,
śreyaḥprāptinimittāya namaḥ somārddhadhāriṇe.

This refers evidently to a personal God, viz. Śiva. The commentator Pārthasārathi himself says that this is a *stuti* addressed to "Viśveśvara Mahādeva"[1], but the verse lends itself, as the scholiast observes to an interpretation, though a strained one, in favour of *Sacrifice.* Kumārila observes that the Mīmāṃsā was reduced to the position of the *lokāyata* system (by Bhartṛmitra and others as Pārthasārathi notes) and he takes the credit of having tried to recover it into the *āstika-patha.*

That Kumārila believed in the Unity of Paramātmā and in the multiplicity of Jīvas, and in the essential identity of the two, we gather from the exposition of his system in the *Sarvasiddhāntasaṅgraha.* It is plainly stated that Ātmā is One as well as many (*bhinnābhinnātmakas tv ātmā*). —One as the Supreme Self and many as the individual selves (*jīvarūpeṇa bhinno 'pi tv abhinnaḥ pararūpataḥ*). The Supreme Self, which alone is eternal, is one and is present in every individual (*asat syāj jīvarūpeṇa sadrūpaḥ pararūpataḥ* and *paramātmā tv anusyūtavṛttir jīve 'pi budhyatām*). This is exactly the teaching of Vedānta. The *Śloka-Vārttika* itself is clear on the point, viz.

1. "*viśveśvaraṃ mahādevaṃ stutipūrvaṃ namasyati.*" Eliot also records the tradition (*Hinduism and Buddhism*, Vol. II, p. 207) that Kumārila was a worshipper of Śiva. This need not militate against the popular belief that he was an incarnation of Kārttikeya (cf. Śaṅkara's *Sarvasiddhāntasaṅgraha*).

where it is stated that the theory of the Self is to be studied in detail in the Vedānta,[1] thereby implying that in this respect the teachings of the two systems are the same. Kumārila's belief in the Unity of the Supreme Self, considered as impersonal, is thus established. As to whether he had any faith in a personal God, of which there seems to be an indication in the first verse of the *Śloka-Vārttika*, opinion differs. But I am inclined to think that he was at heart a believer. Vāsudeva Dīkṣita in his *Kutūhalavṛtti* (Vol.I, p.47) also holds the same opinion regarding Kumārila's belief in God.[2] But God as creator of the Universe he has expressly denied in the *Śloka-Vārttika*.

Kumārila's Date

Although the chronology of Indian History is as a rule the most uncertain and vexed section of Indian Studies, we are not on such uncertain ground in regard to the date of the author of *Tantra-Vārttika*; but it must be confessed that even here there are not lacking difficulties and that our conclusion can only be more or less of the nature of approximation.

The Tibetan Lama Tāra Nātha, in his History of Indian Buddhism, p. 177, note 5, speaks of our author as Gzhon-nu-na-len, which literally rendered is equivalent to "Kumārila." There is evidently no

1. *ity āha nāstikyanirākariṣṇur ātmāstitāṃ bhāṣyakṛd atra yuktyā,*
dṛḍhatvam etadviṣayaś ca bodhaḥ prayāti vedāntaniṣevaṇena.
Śloka-Vārttika, Chowkhamba Sanskrit Series, pp. 727-728.

2. The *Śaṅkara Digvijaya* plainly says that Kumārila confessed before his death that he had been througout his life a believer in God.

doubt that by this name is meant the author of the Mīmāṃsā Vārttika. Tāra Nātha describes him as a contemporary of Srong-tsan-Gampo, who ruled in Tibet in the 7th century (627-650) A.D.

It follows from the tradition referred to above about Kumārila's conversion that his date synchronises with that of Dharmakīrti. We know that Dharmakīrti was the disciple of Dharmapāla, who had been head of the University of Nālandā and the contemporary of Bhartṛhari, the author of *Vākyapadīya*. Dharmapāla was prior to 635 A.D. when Hiuen Tsang visited Nālandā. Dharmakīrti may therefore be assigned to a period after 635 A.D.[1] But he became already famous before 650 A.D. when Srong-tsan-Gampo died. And this supposition is confirmed by the fact that Itsing, who visited India in 671-695 A.D., refers to Dharmakīrti among scholars of late years.[2] It is even likely that during the period when Itsing was travelling through India Dharmakīrti was living.

It is of interest to note that Itsing does not mention the name of Kumārila. But this need not mean that Kumārila lived after Itsing. It seems that Itsing did not care to notice Kumārila

1. Cf. Vidyābhūṣaṇa, *loc. cit.* Dr. Kern holds (*Manual of Indian Buddhism*, p. 130) that Dharmakīrti lived between the stay of Hiuen Tsang, who does not refer to him, and that of Itsing, who speaks of him as a recent celebrity, i.e. about the last quarter of the 7th century.

2. Max Müller (*India : what can it teach us*, pp. 305, 408) was misled by Śivarāma's statement in his Commentary on a passage in the *Vāsavadattā* (viz. *bauddhasaṅgatim ivālaṅkārabhūṣitām*) to hold that Subandhu referred to Dharmakīrti's work. See Kern, *Manual of Indian Buddhism*, p. 130, note 11; Lévi, 'La Date de Candrogomin' in *Bulletin de l'Ecole d'Extreme Orient*, 1903, p. 18; Gray, Introduction to Vāsavadattā (Columbia University Publication), p. 8; Thomas, Introduction to his edition of *Kavivachanasamuccaya*, pp. 47-48.

simply because the latter became a staunch anti-Buddhist. This being so, the silence of Itsing does not militate against the contemporaneity of the two scholars.

Bhavabhūti, who calls himself Kumārila's pupil, lived in the court of Yaśovarmā of Kanauj who flourished about 730 A.D. Assuming that Bhavabhūti was then a man of advanced age, say 50, and that he held his studentship under Kumārila in his early years, it stands to reason that Kumārila may have lived into the beginning of the 8th century. Probably he survived Dharmakīrti, with whom his controversy may be assigned to the end of the 7th century. Dharmakīrti was probably an older contemporary of Kumārila, though he read with the latter in disguise, as tradition has it. Kumārila also read with a Buddhist teacher later on, but the name of this teacher is not known.

The date of Śaṅkarācārya is still a question of dispute. But it is probable that the tradition regarding the interview of Śaṅkara with Kumārila is historically unfounded. The tradition is preserved by both Ānandagiri and Mādhavācārya, the former making Prayāga the place of interview and the latter Rudrapur in Southern India. In his Vārttika on Śaṅkara's *Upadeśa Sāhasrī*, Sureśvara speaks of a verse as borrowed by Śaṅkara from Dharmakīrti. Kumārila was a contemporary of Dharmakīrti and consequently Śaṅkara must have succeeded Kumārila. MM.H.P. Shastri is of opinion that Kumārila preceded Śaṅkara by two generations (Introduction to his edition of *Six Buddhist Nyāya Tracts*), which is not impossible. But the tradition regarding Maṇḍana *versus* Sureśvara, as being once a disciple of Kumārila[1] and then of Śaṅkara, cannot be brushed aside easily. For the two names refer to an identical person. It seems that Śaṅkara was living in the middle or third quarter of the 8th century. The acceptance of 788 A.D. as the date of Śaṅkara's birth would make it difficult to explain how Maṇḍana, who must be dated in the early years of the 8th century, should have been also a pupil of Śaṅkara whose intellectual activities on that supposition must be assigned to the beginning of the 9th century. And the date of Vācaspati being 898 Saṃvat[2] or 841 A.D., it is likely that Śaṅkara preceded him by two or three generations or say about a century.

Kumārila and Prabhākara

Opinion seems to be divided about the chronological relation between Kumārila and Prabhākara. The traditional view is what is recorded in the "Prabhākara School of Pūrva Mīmānsā," which represents Prabhākara as the pupil of Kumārila. This has of course the sanction of *Sarvasiddhānta-saṅgraha*, attributed to the great Śaṅkarācārya,[3] and of Mādhava's *Śaṅkara-digvijaya* (7.77).

1. Both Ānandagiri and Mādhava say that Maṇḍana was Kumārila's principal pupil. As to whether he is to be identified with Bhavabhūti and Bhaṭṭa Umbeka it is hard to say anything correctly in the present stage of our knowledge. See Introduction to Maṇḍana's *Bhāvanāviveka*, Sarasvatī Bhavana Texts, No. 6, published from the Government Sanskrit Library , Benares.

2. This must refer to the Saṃvat Era, for otherwise the interval between Udayana and Vācaspati becomes practically nil.

3. It is difficult to say exactly whether this Śaṅkara is the same as the famous author of the Śārīraka Bhāṣya. That the two were believed to be identical as early as the time of Madhusūdana Sarasvatī (1500-1600 A.D.), whose pupil commented on the *Sarvasiddhāntasaṅgraha*, is no real proof of their identity.

But it has been shown in the *Prabhākara Mīmāṃsā* that considerations of style, etc., would not justify the acceptance of the traditional view as historically sound. And the probability is that Prabhākara was older than Kumārila.

Dr. Keith, who likewise rejects the current view in regard to synchronism of the two authors and their mutual relation, assigns Prabhākara to 600-650 A.D. This is of course on the assumption that Śālikānātha was the pupil of Prabhākara and that he lived before Kumārila. I am afraid both these assumptions are erroneous. That Śālikānātha is of the same school as Prabhākara is undoubted, but there is no proof to show that he was Prabhākara's direct pupil. The statement in Nītipatha, Section 2 of the *Prakaraṇapañcikā*, viz.,

athāsaṃsparśitāśaṅkā yathā śabdasya vāryate,
prabhākaraguroḥ śiṣyais tathā yatno vidhīyate.

(Benares Edition, p.13)

need not imply immediate succession.[1] On the other hand it is very likely, as it has been shown in

1. By way of illustration we may point out that Kāmandaka, who lived about 300 A.D., calls Kauṭilya (400 B.C.) his own *guru,* though there is an interval of no less than 700 years between the dates of the two authors. The second chapter of Kāmandaka's *Nītisāra* deals with the classification of *vidyās* after the manner of the *Vidyāsamuddeśa* section in Kauṭilya's *Arthaśāstra.* The fourth view, therein summed up, is that of Kauṭilya himself as set forth in the Arthaśāstra. Kāmandaka says : *vidyāś catasra evaitā iti no gurudarśanam* (verse 6, p. 27, Trivandrum Edition). The commentator Śaṅkarārya notes in the *Jayamaṅgalā* : *śāstrakārasya kauṭilyo guruḥ.* On the age of Kāmandaka Prof. C. Formici contributed a paper to the 12th International Oriental Congress at Rome (=Alcuni Osservazioni Sull' epoca del Kāmandakīya Nītiśāstra, Bologna, 1899), wherein he tried to show that Kāmandaka was a contemporary of Varāhamihira or even earlier. For Jacobi's views, see his "Zur Frühgeschichte der indischen Philosophie," p. 742. Dr. Frederick ascribed him to a date earlier than 400 A.D. Cf. Sarkar, *The Positive Background of Hindu Sociology,* p. 8.

the Introduction to Varadarāja's Commentary (*Bodhanī*) on the *Nyāyakusumāñjali*,[1] that Śālikānātha was a native of Bengal and belonged to the 10th century A.D., and was presumably an older comtemporary of Udayanācārya. He could not therefore have preceded Kumārila. This date of Śālikā will be quite consistent with the fact of his having quoted from Kumārila's *Ślokavārttika* and referred to Maṇḍana Miśra's *Vidhiviveka.*

But though Śālikā is not prior to Kumārila, Prabhākara's date, as given by Dr. Keith, is by no means affected, for Śālikā was not the immediate successor of Prabhākara.

Pandit S. Kuppuswami Shastri has recently contributed an interesting paper on this vexed question (appearing in the Proceedings of the Second Oriental Conference held at Calcutta pp. 407-412), in which he has sought to defend the traditional view regarding the relation of the two Mīmāṃsā scholars. But I am afraid his argument is not convincing. Vācaspati Miśra speaks in his *Nyāyakaṇikā* of an ancient school of Prabhākara as distinguished from the modern. Vācaspati's time being the middle of the 9th century A.D., we must allow a sufficiently long interval to have already lapsed before Prabhākara's immediate followers could have been rightly denominated as belonging to the "Ancient School."

There is evidently no reference to Kumārila in the expression *vārttikakāra* in the extract quoted from the *Bṛhatī*. This *Vārttikakāra* must have been a predecessor of Kumārila. There existed

1. Introduction (pp. vii-ix) to the 'Kusumāñjalibodhanī', edited by G. N. Kavirāj (*Sarasvatī Bhavan Texts* Series, No. 4, Benares).

at least one Vārttika on the Mīmāṃsā Sūtras before the days of Kumārila, and there is an explicit reference to this in the following passage in the *Tantra-Vārttika* :

sūtreṣv eva hi tat sarvaṃ yad vṛttau yac ca vārtike,
sūtraṃ yonir ihārthānāṃ sarvaṃ sūtre pratiṣṭhitam.
iti ye vadanti tān praty ucyate.
(*Tantra-Vārttika*, Benares Edition, p.606).*

A short history of the Pūrvamīmāṃsāśāstra

I would like to reproduce here a short history of the *Pūrvamīmāṃsā* given by K.S. Rāmaswami Śāstri Śiromaṇi in his Introduction to *Nyāyaratnamālā* of Pārthasārathi Miśra :

The Vedas, consist of two parts : Mantras and Brāhmaṇas. Mantras in each Veda, are generally believed to give advice with reference to the deity, substance of offerings, sacrifices that are already performed, to be attended to and are being performed. Vedic injunctions, basing on these advices, are known as the Brāhmaṇas which give details of sacrifices with the support of the different Mantras. There are several branches or Śākhās in each Veda, and each branch possesses a Mantra and Brāhmaṇa portion where the same sacrifice with different procedures is prescribed. To systematize the different sacrifices as found in the Vedic Śākhās, a vast literature was built up which was known as the Śrautasūtras and was recognised early as the sixth auxiliary to the Vedas. Each

*Kumārila Bhaṭṭa : *Tantravārttika*, a Commentary on Śabara's Bhāṣya on the Pūrvamimāṁsā Sūtras of Jaimini, translated into English by Mahāmahopādhyāya Gaṅgānātha Jhā, M.A., D. Litt., Volume I. Calcutta, 1924 : Introduction, pp. vi-xv.

branch of the Veda had a Śrautasūtra of its own composed by ancient sages. For instance, Āpastamba, and Bodhāyana were the first to fix the methods of the sacrifices with full details in the Yajurveda which were good for the followers of the Taittirīya branch of that Veda.

Thus, the Vedas and the Śrautasūtras combined together form a literature which seeks to supply full details of the Vedic sacrifices. Notwithstanding this vast literature, considerable difficulties arise in understanding the procedure when one begins to perform sacrifices. For instance, the correct interpretation of the Vedic texts and that of the Śrautasūtras, the rules that govern the performances of the rites, the authority of the Vedas that enjoin the sacrifices for conferring different benefits on humanity, and the removal of discrepancies when several ceremonies are to be performed simultaneously,—are some of the questions which are not explained either in the Vedas or in the Śrautasūtras.

The necessity for the Mīmāṃsāśāstra, therefore, arises and this establishes the Vedas being of the supreme authority in determining Dharma or the acts of duty, and helps correctly in interpreting the Vedic texts and so on. Mīmāṃsā decides the exact authorities on Dharma, nature of the rites obtained from different Śākhās with different details, principal and subsidiary parts of a sacrifice, and other allied subjects considered necessary for the sacrificers. Mīmāṃsā or discussion on these rules of Vedic sacrifices originated in very early times, and there were many sages whose views were recorded only by tradition. Jaimini, the author of the Pūrvamīmāṁsāsūtras as available today, mentions many of these sages as taking part in the discussions and contributing their views on particular points.[1] Jaimini, who is generally believed to be disciple of Bādarāyaṇa,[2] is the author of the first twelve chapters of the Pūrvamīmāṃsā, and the subsequent four chapters constituting Saṅkarṣakāṇḍa are also attributed to him, though this is regarded in some quarters as doubtful.[3] Thus, Jaimini is considered to be the author of the Sūtras in sixteen chapters where he has laid down the rules for the Vedic sacrifices, and indicated the method by which Vedic injunctions may be interpreted in case of doubt. The portion of the Veda on which Jaimini carried on discussions in these sixteen chapters is called the Karmakāṇḍa, or the whole of the Veda excepting the Upaniṣads of each Śākhā.

Bādarāyaṇa, who is regarded to be the teacher of Jaimini, had composed sūtras in four chapters and interpreted the Upaniṣad portion of the Vedas so as to reconcile the different philosophical statements contained therein on the question of

1. 1. Bādarāyaṇa 1-1-5; 5-1-19; 6-1-8; 10-8-44; 11-1-64.
   2. Bādari 3-1-3; 8-3-6; 9-2-33.
   3. Atiśāyana 3-2-43; 6-1-6.
   4. Kārṣṇājini 4-3-17; 6-7-35.
   5. Ātreya 4-3-18; 5-2-18.
   6. Āśmarathya 6-5-16.
   7. Āleḳhana 6-5-17.
   8. Lāvukāyana 6-7-37.
   9. Kāmukāyana 11-1-57; 11-1-62. (on page xxi)
2. See Nyāyapariśuddhi p. 285. (on page xxii)
3. Ibid. p. 299 where Kāśakṛtsna is stated as the author of the Saṁkarṣa. Patañjali also states Kāśakṛtsna as the author of Mīmāṃsā. See P. V. Kāṇe's Pūrvamīmāṃsā system. p. 3.

the true knowledge of Brahman. Thus, all the twenty chapters of Mīmāṃsā represent the investigation into the contents of the Vedas, and therefore, all of them are considered to be a part and parcel of the same Śāstra by the ancient commentators. Bodhāyana, Upavarṣa, and Ācārya Sundara Pāṇḍya, the early writers on Mīmāṃsā,[1] are known to have commented on all the twenty chapters, taking for granted that the sole object of the Mīmāṃsā Śāstra is Vedārthavicāra or investigation into the contents of the Vedas, no matter whether it is for Dharma, Devatā or Brahman. It may be said, therefore, that both the Karma and Brahmamīmāṃsās belonged to the same Śāstra; at least, it was considered to be so in ancient days. Thus, it is easy to understand why Jaimini and Bādarāyaṇa frequently quoted each other's views in their respective works.[2] Later on, Bhavadāsa and Devasvāmin commented upon the first sixteen chapters of Jaimini, and thus paved the way for considering the Brahmamīmāṁsā as something separate from the Karmamīmāṁsā[3]. The object of Jaimini's sūtras was said to be the investigation on Dharma and that of Bādarāyaṇa on Brahman. Thus, one common Śāstra of Vedārthavicāra was divided into two distinct Śāstras. Śabarasvāmin, the next commentator, also favoured the same view and his commentary

1. See pp. 465-468 of the Proceedings of the 3rd Oriental Conference. Also see pp. 298-299 of the *Nyāyapariśuddhi* of Vedāntadeśika. For Ācārya Sundara Pāṇḍya see Mm. S. K. Śāstri's paper in *J. O. R.* Madras, Vol. I. P. 1.

2. See p. 8 of the introduction of the *Tattvabindu*. (Annamalai University edition).

3. See *Prapañcahṛdaya*; Trivandrum Sanskrit Series. p. 39.

for 12 chapters alone has come down to us. It appears, however, doubtful whether Śabara commented on the Saṅkarṣasūtras or not.

The period of Śabarasvāmin was the period when the Buddhists came forward with their own advanced tenets which led them to discuss and refute the orthodox systems of philosophy and religion. Great strides were made by them in establishing their favourite theories of Kṣaṇikavāda, Śūnyavāda, Nirālambanavāda, Nairātmya and Vijñānavāda. Destructive criticisms with rational arguments were freely made by the Buddhists in order to destroy the social structure of the community which was based on the Cāturvarṇya system advocated in the Vedic texts. Powerful attacks of the Buddhists on the traditional faith of the people and on the supreme authority of the Vedas, gradually shook the faith of the people in the Vedas and the Vedic sacrifices. Under these threatening circumstances, it fell on the great thinkers of the period like Śabarasvāmin, Vātsyāyana, Praśastapāda, Patañjali, Īśvarakṛṣṇa and others to review and re-establish the six orthodox systems of philosophy on more rational arguments and on absolutely sure grounds to repel the attacks of the Buddhists.

Śabarasvāmin's part was peculiarly difficult and his efforts were particularly strenuous since the Buddhists were specially vehement in their attacks against the Vedas and the Vedic sacrifices. The system of Pūrvamīmāṃsā, moreover, possessed no independent system of philosophy to establish the validity of knowledge derived from the Karmakāṇḍa of the Vedic texts. The Pūrvamīmāṃsā was, therefore, required to be separated from the Uttaramīmāṃsā and had to be given an independent status amongst the orthodox systems of philosophy, with its object to establish Dharma as the chief means of emancipation. In order to raise the Pūrvamīmāṃsā to the status of an independent system, Śabarasvāmin had to go beyond the range of the Sūtras of Jaimini in order to state the Mīmāṃsā-views on all topics and tenets.[1] In his work, he was practically forced to adopt entirely the views stated by Upavarṣa in his commentary on the Bādarāyaṇa Sūtras regarding Ātman[2] and Pramāṇas, and with their help he made an attempt to refute the different schools of Buddhistic thought. The object of the Mīmāṃsāśāstra was narrowed down by him; from Vedārtha it was limited to Dharma alone in the same way as the knowledge of Brahman was the sole object of the other Mīmāṃsā. He introduced several new theories on Bhāvanā, Apūrva, Vākyārthanirṇaya, Nityakāmyaviveka and the theory of knowledge and opened a new school of thought. While

1. See Vṛttikāragrantha of the *Śābarabhāṣya* on 1-1-3. where he has refuted many *vādas* of Buddhists on his own accord. See also Maṇḍana's *Mīmāṃsānukramaṇī* on the same topic :

bahvarthaṃ vaktukāmena tam arthaṃ sautram icchatā,
vṛttikāramateneyaṃ trisūtrī varṇyate 'nyathā.

It is clear from this verse that Śabara's Vṛttikāragrantha contains his own views based on Upavarṣa's Vṛtti on the three sūtras.

2. See Śaṅkara's *Brahmasūtrabhāṣya* 3-3-53 :

nanu śāstramukha eva prathame pāde....dehavyatiriktasyātmano 'stitvam uktam. satyam uktaṃ bhāṣyakṛtā. na tu tatrātmāstitve sūtram asti. iha tu svayam eva sūtrakṛtā tadastitvam ākṣepapurassaraṃ pratiṣṭhāpitam. ita eva cākṛṣya ācāryeṇa śabarasvāminā pramāṇalakṣaṇe varṇitam. ata eva ca bhagavatopavarṣeṇa prathame tantre ātmāstitvābhidhānaprasaktau śārīrake vakṣyāma ity uddhāraḥ kṛtaḥ.

doing so, he attacked the theories of the ancient Vṛttikāras, Bhavadāsa and others.

Bhartṛmitra who followed Śabarasvāmin did not find favour with the innovations introduced by him, and, therefore, made an attempt to uphold the earlier views of the Vṛttikāras in his commentary on the Sūtras.[1]

Kumārilabhaṭṭa, who came later in the field of Mīmāṃsā literature, in his turn, upheld the views of Śabarasvāmin in his commentaries on the *Śābara-bhāṣya* against the views adumbrated by Bhartṛmitra. Kumārila writes in his *Ślokavārttika* that some of the earlier writers had introduced atheism into Mīmāṃsā in many respects and his efforts here are to refute them and to re-establish the Mīmāṃsā as one of the *Āstikadarśanas*.[2] Pārthasārathimiśra informs us further in this connection that Bhartṛmitra and others have propounded the views that actions prescribed or prohibited in the Vedas cannot be capable of producing benefic or malefic results, and that such extraordinary doctrines have been refuted by Kumārila.[3] From these statements of Kumārila and Pārthasārathi, it can be surmised that Bhartṛmitra stood for the old views, and thus came in the way of introducing reforms by later writers like Śabarasvāmin which were necessary in order to save the Śāstra from the attacks of the Buddhists.

The early writers seem to be thoroughly conservative and they expected from all explicit obedience to the Vedic injunctions without expecting

1. See *Ślokavārttika*, pp. 4 and 763.
2. Ibid. p. 4.
3. Ibid.

any result whatever. Vedic injunctions or Niyogas are of three kinds : one prescribes duties to be observed throughout the life-time; the second relates to the rites for obtaining some benefits such as Svarga, Paśu, etc.; while the third prohibits wrong actions. These three kinds are technically known as Nitya, Kāmya and Pratiṣiddha. All these Niyogas or commands from the Vedas should be strictly observed by all and the sundry, simply on the ground that the authority of the Vedas is unquestionable. It is, however, said that in the first and the third kinds of Niyogas no result should be expected as there is hardly any provision for such results in the Vedic sentences. In this respect, the Mīmāṃsā view is identical with that of the atheists because in both, the life-long performance of Vedic rites is incapable of conferring any beneficial result. Even so, the actions that are prohibited in the Vedas cannot be calculated to produce any harm whatsoever. The atheists hold the view above stated, as they do not believe in the next birth, nor in the existence of the soul which is supposed to transmigrate. The reason for the Mīmāṃsakas holding the same view, is that the Vedic Niyogas being supreme commands require to be obeyed, no matter whether they give rise to good or bad results or no result. Even those Niyogas which seem to have been prescribed for the fulfilment of certain desires such as Svarga or Paśu should be obeyed since they are Vedic commands while the desired results are obtained automatically. Similarly there are many other instances where the early Mmīāṃsakas were very strict in preserving the authority of the Vedas.[1]

Śabarasvāmin and Kumārilabhaṭṭa, being of a reformative tendency, were not in favour with these ancient theories which failed to satisfy them. On the contrary, they sought to establish that there is no difference between Vedic and non-Vedic injunctions.[2]

None is likely to undertake an action without knowing the result, particularly in non-Vedic injunctions. Even so is the case with the Vedic injunctions. There ought to be some expectation of results, otherwise none is likely to obey the Vedic injunctions or undertake to perform rituals.[3] They, thus, formulated that no Vedic injunction would be complete without indicating the result to be expected, and the means and methods to be adopted for its realisation.[4] Moreover, according to Kumārila, it is the knowledge of Dharma and not the Vedārthavicāra that is considered to be the supreme goal.[5] He, therefore, tried to establish that each Dharma based on Vedic

1. For instance, the Niyogavākyārthavāda, Kāryaparavākyavāda, Akhyātivāda, Śrutiviruddhasmṛtiprāmāṇyaniṣedha etc. may be cited in this respect.

2. See the Bhāṣya and Vārttika on the first and second *sūtra* of Jaimini, where a comparison on Vedic and non-Vedic sentences is made.

3. *sarvasyaiva hi śāstrasya karmaṇo vāpi kasya cit,*
yāvat prayojanaṃ noktaṃ tāvat tat kena gṛhyate. (S.V.p.)
prayojanam anuddiśya na mando 'pi pravartate. Ibid. p. 653

4. See Bhāṣya on the following Adhikaraṇas : 6-1-1; 4-3-5; 4-3-6; 7-1-1-; 9-1-1; 2-1-2; 11-1-4. See also :
tasmāt prakrāntarūpo 'pi vidhis tāvat pratīkṣate,
yāvad yogyatvam āpannā bhāvanānyānapekṣiṇī.
ekabhāvanayopāttās trayo 'py aṃśāḥ parasparam.
upakāryopakāritvaṃ paścād anubhavanti te. S.V. 7.276; 265.

5. Ibid. p. 4.

injunctions does confer a specific result.[1] Reforms of this kind were introduced by Kumārilabhaṭṭa on the lines of Śabara and he adversely criticised the old method of the Vṛttikāras and Bhartṛmitra. No wonder that Kumārilabhaṭṭa should be considered as one of the greatest reformers in the domain of Vedic thought, especially as embodied in the Karmakāṇḍa.[2] He may also be called the saviour of the Vedic religion which was almost tottering under the onslaught of the celebrated Buddhist scholars such as Diṅnāga and Dharmakīrti. He boldly declared that Dharma should be learnt only from the Vedas and the 14 Vidyāsthānas supported by the Vedas, and not from any other source such as the works of the Buddhists and the Jainas which deny the supreme authority of the Vedas.[3] He did not follow the Niyogavākyārthavāda or Kāryavākyārthavāda but established the Bhāvanāvākyārthavāda as suggested earlier by Śabarasvāmin.

Prabhākara, another very celebrated thinker of the period appeared after Kumārila, and it is said that he received direct instructions from Kumārilabhaṭṭa. Nevertheless, he totally differed from his preceptor and predecessor and was not in favour with his reforms and deviations from the early writers. He re-established the views of Bhartṛmitra on the Niyogas of Nitya and Niṣiddha duties already referred to, and accepted Vedārthavicāra as the sole purpose of Mīmāṃsā, as

1. *mokṣārthī na pravarteta tatra kāmyaniṣiddhayoḥ, nityanaimittike kuryāt pratyavāyajihāsayā.* Ibid. 5-110.
2. See *Tantravārttika* 1-3-2.
3. Ibid. 1-3-3.

inculcated by the old Vṛttikāras like Bodhāyana and others. He upheld the Niyogavākyārthavāda, Kāryaparavākyavāda, Anvitābhidhānavāda and Akhyātivāda in consonance with the orthodox views on Mīmāmsā. He opposed all reforms introduced in the five Vārttikas by Kumārila on the Śābarabhāṣya. In doing so, Prabhākara did not directly quote Kumārila's passages for the purpose of refutation but instead, following in the footsteps of Kumārila, he refuted him, while commenting on the Śabara's Bhāṣya itself, often twisting the original sentences so as to suit his own purpose.[1] His followers, on the other hand, had supplied the necessary information wherever he meant to refute the views of Kumārila. Prabhākara commanded great respect and prominence in the field of Mīmāmsā because of his adopting an indirect method in rejecting the innovations of Kumārila and also because he had anticipated his own views from the Bhāṣya of Śabara as if they were the views of Śabara himself. In the above manner, the Bhāṣya of Śabara was interpreted by two eminent scholars—Kumārila and Prabhākara, equally staunch followers of the new and old schools of Mīmāmsā.

Maṇḍanamiśra, who is believed to be another disciple of Kumārila was, however, true to his preceptor and condemned the methods of Prabhākara. He established in his works, *Vidhiviveka*,

1. Compare *Bṛhatī* of Prabhākara on the following Bhāṣyas :—

Jijñāsādhikaraṇa :— *dṛṣṭo hi tasyārthaḥ karmāvabodhanaṃ nāma. kiṃ paraś ceti. kva puruṣaparatvaṃ kva vā puruṣo guṇabhūtaḥ. sa hi niḥśreyasena puruṣaṃ saṃyunakti. anarthaṃ ca ṛcchet.*

Codanādhikaraṇa :—*codaneti kriyāyāḥ pravartakaṃ vacanam āhuḥ. śaknoty avagamayitum. yo yāgam anutiṣṭhati taṃ dhārmika iti. śreyaskaraḥ. ko 'rthaḥ yo niḥśreyasāya. ko 'narthaḥ yaḥ pratyavāyāya.* —and so on.

Bhāvanāviveka, *Vibhramaviveka* and *Brahmasiddhi* all the reforms introduced by Kumārila with some modifications being the results of his own independent thinking. Kumārila seems to have excited a desire for independent thinking on the part of his disciples, by his own example of reforming the old school of Mīmāmsā. It is for this reason that we find his disciples Maṇḍana and Umbeka, at times, differing from him. Umbeka, otherwise known as Bhavabhūti, is said to have written a commentary on Kumārila's *Ślokavārttika* where he also introduced certain deviations from Kumārila.

Śālikānātha is the celebrated follower of the Prābhākara system, and he appeared after Maṇḍana. He is believed to be a disciple of Prabhākara himself. He, in his turn, commented upon the Bṛhatī and the Laghvī of Prabhākara, and very ably established the views of his teacher. He quoted from all the Vārttikas of Kumārila wherever Prabhākara differed from him and made an able attempt to show that the Bhāṣya of Śabarasvāmin favours only the theories of Prabhākara and not those of Kumārila. He wrote also several independent works[1] in which he tried to show that the views of Kumārila were not based on the Bhāṣya and that the views of Prabhākara and the orthodox methods he followed, were adopted by Śabara in his Bhāṣya. He ably replied to the criticisms of Maṇḍana on Prabhākara's Kāryavākyārthavāda,[2] and supported the Akhyātivāda of Prabhākara against all other systems of philosophy

1. *Prakaraṇapañcikā* and *Mīmāṃsābhāṣyapariśiṣṭa*.

2. See *Ṛjuvimalā* pp. 20, 24 (Madras edition).

such as the Nyāya-vaiśeṣika, Mīmāṃsā of Bhāṭṭa and the Vedānta.

Thus, in the course of time, the ancient system of Mīmāṃsā, taking its origin from thinkers like Jaimini, Upavarṣa and others, was forgotten, and it divided itself into two distinct schools, antagonistic to each other, known as the Bhāṭṭa and the Prābhākara schools of Mīmāmsā, though both relied on the same source, namely the Bhāṣya of Śabarasvāmin.

It may be pointed out that during this period the great Śaṅkarācārya flourished and wrote his immortal Bhāṣyas on the Upaniṣads and the Bādarāyaṇasūtras. He was guided mostly by the views of Kumārila in his statements regarding the Mīmāṃsā system. He believed in the separation of the two systems of Pūrva and Uttara Mīmāṃsās[1] as these had different objects, namely, the Dharma and Brahman. He thought that Śabarasvāmin was right in making the Pūrvamīmāṃsā a separate school of philosophy in order to defend the Vedic religion against the attacks of the Buddhists. He believed that it was Śabara and Kumārila who made his way easy in establishing the Advaitism as the philosophy of the Upaniṣads against the contending Buddhists. He was disposed to think that Kumārila was right in his interpretation of the Śābarabhāṣya with reference to the Bhāvanāvākyārthavāda, Nityakāmyaviveka, Abhihitānvayavāda and the theory of knowledge. He was visibly not in favour with the theories of Prabhākara and his interpretations

1. See 1.1.1. of his *Bhāṣya* on the *Bādarāyaṇasūtra*.

of the Śābarabhāṣya. His was an attitude of compromise between the two conflicting parties, namely, the Mīmāṃsakas and the Buddhists. Śaṅkara not only pointed out the evil arising out of a blind faith in the Vedic sacrifices but also warned the people against the dangers of following the purely rationalistic philosophy of the Buddhists.

Vācaspatimiśra was the next great writer on all the Brahmanical systems of philosophy, and pleaded for an independent status for every one of them. He upheld the Bhāṭṭa school of Mīmāṃsā on the lines of Maṇḍanamiśra. He answered all the charges made against Maṇḍana by Śālikānātha, and condemned the views of Prabhākara which were not supported by Śabarasvāmin. It was a common practice of scholars in those days to oppose or support either of the two schools of Mīmāṃsā, and thus we come across several works dealing with the Mīmāṃsā system. Authors such as Mahodadhi, Mahāvrata etc. are known to have written works in support of either of these schools,[1] though their works still remain to be discovered. In the last phase, the two schools were supported by two great figures, namely Bhavanātha and Pārthasārathimiśra. Bhavanātha, in his work *Nayaviveka*, written in the concise form of Adhikaraṇa without reference to the *sūtras* of Jaimini, sought to establish the views of Prabhākara, and actually supplied all instances where Prabhākara deviated from the path of Kumārila. From Śālikānātha and Bhavanātha we can easily under-

1. Vide. *J.O.R.* Madras, vol. II pp. 62-64.

stand that Prabhākara was later than Kumārila. It also appears from their testimony that Prabhākara refuted the views of Kumārila inculcated in his *Bṛhaṭṭīkā* which is now no longer extant, but the existence of which can be proved by the numerous quotations preserved in the philosophical literature.

Pārthasārathimiśra in his four works on Mīmāṃsā followed the Bhāṭṭa school, and vehemently opposed the other system. The object of writing these works appears to be to show on the one hand that Prabhākara was not correct in saying that his views were supported by the text of Śabara's *Bhāṣya*, and, on the other, to prove that Kumārila was correct in interpreting the *Bhāṣya* and in recording what was meant by Śabarasvāmin. *Nyāyaratnamālā* is the work where Pārthasārathi freely discusses the merits of the arguments of both the parties, and delivers his own considered judgement thereon.*

***Nyāyaratnamālā* of Pārthasārathimiśra with the commentary of Rāmānujācārya entitled the *Nāyakaratna*, critically edited with an introduction and Indices by K. S. Rāmaswami Śāstri, Śiromaṇi Śrauta Paṇḍit, Oriental Institute, Baroda, 1937 : Introduction, pp. xx-xxix.

FROM THE ŚLOKAVĀRTTIKA

Two hundred and twenty four *kārikās* have truly been selected from the *Ślokavārttika*. These *kārikās* have generally been quoted by many authors in their works. I have also included here such *kārikās*, which, according to my opinion are worth quoting. For page references, the reader is requested to consult Chowkhamba-Sanskrita-Granthamālā (granthasaṃkhyā 3) Mīmāṃsāślokavārttikam—Śrīmat Kumārilabhaṭṭaviracitam, nikhilatantraparatantraśrīmatpārthasārathimiśrapraṇitayā Nyāyaratnākarākhyayā vyākhyayānugatam / Vārāṇasīyarājakīyapradhāna-sanskritapāṭhaśālāyāṃ sāhityaśāstrādhyāpakena Mānavallyupāhva-Tailaṅga Rāmaśāstriṇā sapariṣkāraṃ pariśodhitam / Kāśyām (=Benares), A.D. 1898, Vikrama era 1955.

atītānāgate 'py arthe sūkṣme vyavahite 'pi ca,
pratyakṣaṁ yogināṃ iṣṭam kaiś cin muktātmanām api.
141.1

atyantāsaty api jñānam arthe śabdaḥ karoti hi,
tenotsarge sthite tasya doṣābhāvāt pramāṇatā.
46.5

atvam ity ucyamānaṃ hi na dīrghaplutayor bhavet,
ātvaṃ ca hrasvaplutayos traimātryaṃ na ca pūrvayoḥ.
521.3

atha pūrvāparāsattvaṃ hetus tatrāpy asiddhatā,
sann eva sādhanābhāvāc chabdo naivopalabhyate.
740.1

athavā vāsanaivāstu saṃskāraḥ sarva eva hi,
dṛḍhajñānagṛhīte 'rthe saṃskāro 'stīti manyate.
535.6

athāśubhād vinā sṛṣṭiḥ sthitir vā nopapadyate,
ātmādhīnābhyupāye hi bhavet kiṃ nāma dūṣakam.
653.1

aniṣyamāṇe sāmānye vṛttiḥ śabdānumānayoḥ,
naiva syān na hi saṃbandho bhedair ānantyato bhavet.
555.5

antyavarṇe 'pi vijñāte pūrvasaṃskārakāritam,
smaraṇaṃ yaugapadyena sarveṣv anye pracakṣate.
538.7

anyathāpy upapannatvād iyaṃ pravacanādinā,
na śaktā kartṛmūlāya prokte ca smaraṇaṃ sthitam.
951.5

anyenopaplave 'bhīṣṭe dvaitavādaḥ prasajyate,
svābhāvikīm avidyāṃ tu nocchettuṃ kaś cid arhati.
663.3

aparāmṛśyamāne 'pi svāpakāle sukhāśraye,
saṃbhoge mṛduśayyādau prāk pravṛttiś ca dṛśyate.
693.1

abhāvasya ca yo 'bhāvaḥ sa ca tasmād vilakṣaṇaḥ,
bhāva eva bhaven no ced gaur agaus te prasajyate.
591.3

abhāvam eva nañ prāha vartamānādikālikam,
nāmadhātvarthayogī ca niṣedho 'nyārthabhāk bhavet.
930.3

abhāvāc cānukampyānāṃ nānukampāsya jāyate,
sṛjec ca śubham evaikam anukampāprayojitaḥ.
651.5

abhāvo vā pramāṇena svānurūpeṇa mīyate,
prameyatvād yathā bhāvas tasmād bhāvātmakāt pṛthak.
491.5

aśābde cāpi vākyārthe na padārtheṣv aśābdatā,
vākyārthasyeva naiteṣāṃ nimittāntarasaṃbhavaḥ.
909.3

aśeṣakarmanāśe vā punaḥ sṛṣṭir na yujyate,
karmaṇāṃ vāpy abhivyaktau kiṃ nimittaṃ tadā bhavet.
658.3

asatā yat tu sādṛśyam asataḥ parikalpyate,
dhruvaṃ śaśaviṣāṇena kharaśṛṅgasya tad bhavet.
882.3

asaty api ca bāhye 'rthe vākyārthapratibhā yathā,
padārthe 'pi tathaiva syāt kim apohaḥ prakalpyate.
577.3

asattve ye ca dṛṣṭāntāḥ prakṛtipratyayādayaḥ,
asiddhās te yato loke tatsadbhāvaḥ pratīyate.
889.5

asti hy ālocanājñānaṃ prathamaṃ nirvikalpakam,
bālamūkādivijñānasadṛśaṃ śuddhavastujam.
168.4

ahaṃ vedmīty ahaṃbuddhir jñātāram abhigacchati,
tatra syād jñātṛvijñānaṃ tadādhāro 'thavā pumān.
717.1

ātmalābhe ca bhāvānāṃ kāraṇāpekṣatā bhavet,
labdhātmanāṃ svakāryeṣu pravṛttiḥ svayam eva tu.
60.1

ātmā jñātavya ity etan mokṣārthaṃ na ca coditam,
karmapravṛttihetutvam ātmajñānasya lakṣyate.
669.3

ādhārātmani vijñāte sukham ādheyabodhanam,
tasyaiva tāvat prastāvād atha gaur ity ato 'bravīt.
510.5

ānupūrvī ca varṇānāṃ hrasvadīrghaplutāś ca ye,
kālasya pravibhāgās tair jāyante dhvanyupādhayaḥ.
806.5

ikārapariṇāmena yakāraḥ kriyatām iti,
siddhe śabdārthasaṃbandhe tac chāstraṃ hi pravartate.
782.1

idaṃ puṇyam idaṃ pāpaṃ ity etasmin padadvaye,
ācaṇḍālaṃ manuṣyāṇām alpaṃ śāstraprayojanam.[1]
209.1

īśvarecchā yadīṣyeta saiva syāl lokakāraṇam,
īśvarecchāvaśitve hi niṣphalā karmakalpanā.
658.5

1. In the previous kārikā, Kumārilabhaṭṭa attributes this to Vyāsa. But this appears as 1.40 in the *Vākyapadīya* of Bhartṛhari.

uptamātre na hi vrīhau phalam utpadyate kva cit,
athāṅkuro 'pi tatra syāt svargo 'py astīti gamyatām.
682.9

ekaṃ ced grāhakaṃ grāhyaṃ kuto bhinnatvavāg iyam,
bhinnaṃ cet katham ucyeta tasyaikatvaṃ punas tvayā.
302.7

ekena tu pramāṇena sarvajño yena kalpyate,
nūnaṃ sa cakṣuṣā sarvān rasādīn pratipadyate.
80.1

evaṃ dīrghādayaḥ sarve dhvanidharmā iti sthitam,
nādo vāyuguṇas tadvān vāyur vā yadi kalpyate.
786.1

evaṃ dhvaniguṇān sarvān nityatvena vyavasthitān,
varṇā anupatantaḥ syur arthabhedāvabodhinaḥ.
806.3

evaṃ padārthavākyārthasaṃghātair upakalpitām,
viśiṣṭāṃ bhāvanāṃ prāpya vṛttir vidhiniṣedhayoḥ.
921.3

evam evāśvakarṇādau samudāyaprasiddhitaḥ,
vāryate 'vayavasyārtho vṛkṣādyarthāvadhāraṇāt.
908.1

kathaṃ vā vastv apohyeta nābhāvo bhāvam ṛcchati,
apohyamāne cābhāve bhāva evāvaśiṣyate.
582.5

kartṛtvam eva kāṣṭhāder āpannaṃ devadattavat,
dhātunoktakriye nityaṃ kārake kartṛteṣyate.
865.7

karmajanyopabhogārthaṃ śarīraṃ na pravartate,
tadabhāve na kaś cid dhi hetus tatrāvatiṣṭhate.
671.3

kalpanīyāś ca sarvajñā bhaveyur bahavas tava,
ya eva syād asarvajñaḥ sa sarvajñaṃ na budhyate.
86.3

kasmāt sāsnādimatsv eva gotvaṃ yasmāt tadātmakam,
tādātmyam asya kasmāc cet svabhāvād iti gamyatām.
557·5
kasya cid dhetumātratvaṃ yady adhiṣṭhātṛteṣyate,
karmabhiḥ sarvajīvānāṃ tatsiddheḥ siddhasādhanam.
659·5
kāryārthāpattigamyaṃ naḥ śrotraṃ pratinaraṃ sthitam,
yady api vyāpi caikaṃ ca tathāpi dhvanisaṃskṛtiḥ.
747·5
kālaś caiko vibhur nityaḥ pravibhakto 'pi gamyate
varṇavat sarvabhāveṣu vyajyate kena cit kva cit.
806.7
kīdṛg gavaya ity evaṃ pṛṣṭo nāgarikair yadi,
bravīty āraṇyako vākyaṃ yathā gaur gavayas tathā.
433·9
ke cid āhur asadrūpam aṃśatvaṃ tu na vāryate,
sārūpyam eva sāmānyaṃ piṇḍānāṃ yena kalpyate.
563·1
krīḍārthāyāṃ pravṛttau ca vihanyeta kṛtārthatā,
bahuvyāparatāyāṃ ca kleśo bahutaro bhavet.
653·7
kṣaṇabhaṅgo ghaṭādīnāṃ vāryas tair eva sādhanaiḥ,
tathaiva pratyabhijñānād yāvad dṛṣṭaṃ na bādhate.
839·7
kṣaṇikaṃ sādhanaṃ cāsya buddhir apy anuvartate,
meghāndhakāraśarvaryāṃ vidyujjanitadṛṣṭivat.
740·3
gakārādiṣu sāmānyaṃ śabdatvaṃ kalpyate yathā,
gotvaṃ ca śābaleyādau tathaitat kiṃ na kalpyate.
515·1
gṛhītvā vastusadbhāvaṃ smṛtvā ca pratiyoginam,
mānasaṃ nāstitājñānaṃ jāyate 'kṣānapekṣaṇāt.
482.1

gośabda iti vijñānam anvayavyatirekajam,
tasmād gamakataivādāv abhidhāyakatā punaḥ.

505.7

granthādhyayanavelāyāṃ svarūpeṇāvadhāraṇam,
pradhānaṃ padavarṇānāṃ vicchinnānām upāśritam.

887.3

ghaṭāyonmīlitaṃ cakṣuḥ paṭaṃ na hi na budhyate,
etad eva prasaktavyaṃ viṣayasyāpi saṃskṛtau.

746.1

citrabuddhyānayā bhrāntyā varṇebhyo vyatirekataḥ,
paścād gaur iti vijñānaṃ pratyakṣaṃ kaiś cid iṣyate.

539.7

citrarūpāṃ ca tāṃ buddhiṃ sadasadvarṇagocarām,
ke cid āhur yathā varṇo gṛhyate 'ntyaḥ pade pade.

538.5

chedane khadiraprāpte palāśe na cchidā yathā,
tathaiva paraśor loke chidayā saha naikatā.

157.4

jātim evākṛtiṃ prāhur vyaktir ākriyate yayā,
sāmānyaṃ tac ca piṇḍānāṃ ekabuddhinibandhanam.

546.1

jāter astitvanāstitve na ca kaś cid vivakṣati,
nityatvāl lakṣyamāṇāyā vyaktes te hi viśeṣaṇe.

932.7

jātyā yathā ghaṭādīnāṃ vyavahāropalakṣaṇam,
tathaiva cānupūrvyāder jātidvāreṇa setsyati.

804.3

jijñāsyaḥ saṃśayād dharmaḥ śreyaskaratayāpi ca,
asaṃdigdho hy ajijñāsyo yo vā syān niṣprayojanaḥ.

42.3

jñātavān aham evedaṃ puredānīṃ ca vedmy aham,
tasya jñānakṣaṇaḥ ko nu viṣayaḥ parikalpyatām.

719.3

jñātā ca kas tadā tasya yo janān bodhayiṣyati,
upalabdher vinā caitat katham adhyavasīyatām.
651.1

jñānaṃ jñānam itīdaṃ tu na dvayor anuvartate
vyatiriktaṃ tu sāmānyaṃ tvayā nābhyupagamyate.
304.3

jñānaṃ mokṣanimittaṃ ca gamyate nendriyādinā,
na ca sāṃkhyādivijñānaṃ mokṣo vedena codyate.
669.1

jñānaśaktisvabhāvo 'to nityaḥ sarvagataḥ pumān.
dehāntarakṣamaḥ kalpyaḥ so 'gacchann eva yokṣyate.
707.1

jñāpakatvād dhi saṃbandhaḥ svātmajñānam apekṣate,
tenāsau vidyamāno 'pi nāgṛhītaḥ prakāśakaḥ.
647.7

tato gaur iti sāmānyaṃ vācyam ekaṃ na sidhyati,
jātyantaramatiś caiṣu bhavej jātyantareṣv iva.
581.5

tato vedānusāreṇa kāryā dikśrotratāmatiḥ,
diśaḥ śrotram iti hy etat pralayeṣv abhidhīyate.
768.1

tatra jñātātmatattvānāṃ bhogāt pūrvakriyākṣaye,
uttarapracayāsattvād deho notpadyate punaḥ.
671.1

tatra bāhyārthaśūnyatvaṃ tulyaṃ tāvad dvayor api,
nivṛttyāsya tato jñāne tadvat saṃvṛtikalpanā.
220.9

tatra mlecchādivat sarve karmākṛtvāpi vaidikam,
phalaṃ labhanta ity evaṃ naṣṭā vedapramāṇatā.
685.5

tatrārthaśūnyaṃ vijñānaṃ yogācāraḥ samāśritaḥ,
tasyāpy abhāvam icchanti ye mādhyamikavādinaḥ.
220.7

tathā cāpekṣamāṇasya svātantryaṃ pratihanyate,
jagac cāsṛjatas tasya kiṃ nāmeṣṭaṃ na sidhyati.
653.3

tathānvākhyānabhedena prakṛtipratyayādibhiḥ,
nāmākhyātavyavasthānaṃ smaraṇenopalabhyate.
897.5

tathāpi yat kriyā tasyām upakāryopakāritā,
sa kriyāsaṃgateḥ paścāt saṃbandhaḥ kriyate tayoḥ.
502.3

tathā vegena dhāvanto nāvy ārūḍhāś ca gacchataḥ,
parvatādīn vijānanti bhramena bhramataś ca tān.
520.3

tathaiva nityacaitanyāḥ pumāṃso dehavṛttayaḥ,
gṛhṇanti karaṇānītān rūpādīn dhīr asau matā.
834.5

tadbhedāc chrutibhedaś ca pratiśrotṛvyavasthitaḥ,
nāvaśyaṃ śrotram ākāśam asmābhiś cābhyupeyate.
747.1

tasmāc chotraparicchinno yady arthaṃ gamayen na vā,
sarvathā tasya śabdatvaṃ lokasiddhaṃ na hīyate.
511.7

tasmāt prāg api sarve 'mī sraṣṭur āsan padādayaḥ,
syāt tatpūrvakatā cāsya caitanyād asmadādivat.
673.7

tasmād akṛtrimaḥ śabdo na kadā cid vinaśyati,
nityena nityasaṃbandhād ākāśaparamāṇuvat.
822.3

tasmād acalato 'pi syāc calane kartṛtātmanaḥ,
yathaivābhidyamānasya devadattasya bhettṛtā.
710.9

tasmād ananumānatvaṃ śabde pratyakṣavad bhavet,
trairūpyarahitatvena tādṛgviṣayavarjanāt.
430.5

tasmād asattve sattve vā saṃbandhasya yad eva naḥ,
jāyetābhaṅguraṃ jñānaṃ tasyaiva syāt pramāṇatā.
471.8

tasmād asatyahetor yā paramārthe matis tava,
sāpy asatyā na satyaṃ hi satyābhāsena gamyate.
256.2

tasmād uccāraṇaṃ tasya mātrākālaṃ pratīyate,
dvimātraṃ vā trimātraṃ vā na varṇo mātrikaḥ kva cit.
522.3

tasmād ubhayahānena vyāvṛttyanugamātmakaḥ,
puruṣo 'bhyupagantavyaḥ kuṇḍalādiṣu sarpavat.
695.7

tasmād yatrobhayor doṣaḥ parihāro 'pi vā samaḥ,
naikaḥ paryanuyoktavyas tādṛgarthavicāraṇe.
341.7

tasmād yathā mahāvākye laghūnām anirākriyā,
tathaiva padavarṇānāṃ nāsattvaṃ vākyabuddhiṣu.
886.1

tasmān na padadharmo 'sti vināśī kaś cid īdṛśaḥ,
tena nityaṃ padaṃ siddhaṃ varṇanityatvavādinām.
807.3

tasmān na paramāṇvāder ārambhaḥ syāt tadicchayā,
puruṣasya ca śuddhasya nāśuddhā vikṛtir bhavet.
662.3

tena jñānāntaraṃ vā syād grāhyam ātmāṃśa eva vā,
svarūpaviparītaṃ ca kathaṃ grāhyaṃ pratīyate.
307.7

tena sārūpyaśabdena kiṃ punaḥ pratipadyate,
samānarūpabhāvaś cej jātiḥ sāsmābhir iṣyate.
563.3

tenātmadharmo bhedānām ekadhīviṣayo 'sti naḥ,
sāmānyam ākṛtir jātiḥ śaktir vā so 'bhidhīyatām.
550.3

tenaikatvena varṇasya buddhir ekopajāyate,
viśeṣabuddhisadbhāvo bhaved vyañjakabhedataḥ.
515.7

triguṇaḥ paudgalo vāyam ākāśasyātha vā guṇaḥ,
varṇād anyo 'tha nādātmā vāyurūpo 'rthavācakaḥ.
811.1

dhārmikādhārmikatvābhyāṃ pīḍānugrahakāriṇau,
prasiddhau hi tathā cāha pārāśaryo 'tra vastuni.
208.6

na ca vyañjakabhedena deśabhedopalambhanam,
pradīpair bhinnadeśasthair na bhinno vyajyate ghaṭaḥ.
733.1

na ca sarvātmanākṣeṇa saṃbandho 'rthasya vidyate,
yena sarvāvabodhaḥ syāt tatpramāṇābhidhāyinām.
153.2

na cānanuṣṭhito dharmo nānuṣṭhānam ṛte mateḥ,
na ca vedād ṛte sā syād vedo na ca padādibhiḥ.
673.5

na cānavayavaṃ vyoma jainasāṃkhyaniṣedhataḥ,
tenākāśaikadeśo vā yad vā vastvantaraṃ bhavet.
747.3

na cāpi vāsanābhedād bhedaḥ sadrūpatāpi vā,
apohānāṃ prakalpyeta na hy avastuni vāsanā.
592.2

na cāvastuna ete syur bhedās tenāsya vastutā,
kāryādīnām abhāvaḥ ko yo 'bhāvaḥ kāraṇādinaḥ.
474.8

na cāsti vāsanābhedo nimittāsaṃbhavāt tava,
jñānabhedo nimittaṃ cet tasya bhedaḥ kathaṃ punaḥ
260.7

na bhinnaḥ kālabhedena tathā śabdo na deśataḥ,
paryāyād avirodhaś ced vyāpitvād api dṛśyatām.
780.7

.nuñcanti sāmarthyaṃ vākyārtheṣu padāni naḥ,
ˏ,ıātrāvasiteṣv eṣu padārthebhyaḥ sa gamyate.
909.1

ıy amūrtasya sadbhāvo mūrtamadhye vihanyate,
:a kuḍyādibhir vyoma nāśyate sāryate 'pi vā.
755.5

ıumānāvagamyaṃ tat pratyakṣe lakṣaṇena kim,
.bhāvikaś ca saṃbandho jātivyaktyor na hetumān.
553.3

ıdhāreṇa vinā sṛṣṭir ūrṇanābher apīṣyate,
prāṇināṃ bhakṣaṇāc cāpi tasya lālā pravartate.
651.3

nāmadhātvarthayogī ca naiva nañ pratiṣedhakaḥ,
vadato 'brāhmaṇādharmāv anyamātravirodhinau.
575.5

nārthasya vācakaḥ sphoṭo varṇebhyo vyatirekataḥ,
ghaṭādivan na dṛṣṭena virodho dharmasiddhitaḥ.
543.4

nityasya nitya evārthaḥ kṛtakasyāpramāṇatā,
unmattavacanatvaṃ tu pūrvam eva nirākṛtam.
955.2

nityān śabdārthasaṃbandhān āśrityoktena hetunā,
svataḥprāmāṇyasiddhyartham aprāmāṇye nirākṛte.
498.5

nityeṣu satsu varṇeṣu vyavahārāt kramodayaḥ,
ghaṭādiracanā yadvan nityeṣu paramāṇuṣu.
803.1

nirviśeṣaṃ na sāmānyaṃ bhavec chaśaviṣāṇavat,
sāmānyarahitatvāc ca viśeṣās tadvad eva hi.
548.1

niṣpannā eva dṛśyante vyāpārāḥ sarva eva hi,
sūkṣmā vyāpārabhedās tu dṛśyante na kadācana.
529.7

naiva vā grahaṇaṃ teṣā śabdeṃ buddhis tu tadv
saṃskārānukṛteḥ so 'pi mahattvādy avabuddhy
51

padavākyātmakaḥ sphoṭaḥ sārūpyānyanivartan
eteṣāṃ astv anityatvaṃ nāsmākaṃ teṣu nityatā
811.3

padārthapūrvakas tasmād vākyārtho 'yam avasthitaḥ,
artharūpaṃ ivāpannaṃ vākyaṃ vākyasya gocaraḥ.
941.1

padārthamātram eveṣṭaṃ viśeṣe 'vagate kva cit,
padaṃ prayuñjate ke cid varṇaṃ vārthasamanvitam.
887.1

padārthā gamayanty etaṃ pratyekaṃ saṃśaye sati,
sāmastye nirṇayotpādāt sthāṇumūrdhasthakākavat.
948.5

padārthānugataś caiṣa vākyārtho gamyate sadā,
na viśiṣṭārthatā tasmād vākyasvātantryasādhinī.
908.7

padāvadhāraṇopāyān bahūn icchanti sūrayaḥ,
kramanyūnātiriktatvasvaravākyasmṛtiśrutīḥ.
896.3

parasparānapekṣāś ca śrotrabuddhyā svarūpataḥ,
varṇā evāvagamyante na pūrvāparavastuni.
512.7

paśyataḥ śvetimārūpaṃ hreṣāśabdaṃ ca śṛṇvataḥ,
khuranikṣepaśabdaṃ ca śveto 'śvo dhāvatīti dhīḥ.
947.1

pīno divā na bhuṅkte cety evamādivacaḥśrutau,
rātribhojanavijñānaṃ śrutārthāpattir iṣyate.
463.5

pumān akartā yeṣāṃ tu teṣām api guṇaiḥ kriyā,
katham ādau bhavet tatra karma tāvan na vidyate.
664.1

pṛthaṅ na copalabhyante varṇasyāvayavāḥ kva cit,
na ca varṇeṣv anusyūtā dṛśyante tantuvat paṭe.
513.2

prakṛtipratyayau yadvad apekṣete parasparam,
padaṃ padāntaraṃ yadvad vākyaṃ vākyāntaraṃ tathā.
918.1

pratijñāpūrvasaṃjalpasarvalokaprasiddhataḥ,
yāvajjīvam ahaṃ maunīty uktimātreṇa bādhyate.
366.2

pratyuccāraṇanirvṛttir bhāṣya eva nirākṛtā,
sargādau ca kriyā nāsti tādṛk kālo hi neṣyate.
469.7f.

pratyekaṃ cāpy aśaktānāṃ samudāye 'py aśaktatā,
tatra yaḥ parihāras te sa no 'trāpi bhaviṣyati.
533.8

pramāṇābhāvatas tena jñānāstitvādi durlabham,
sarvaṃ cāpy asmadādīnāṃ mithyā jñānaṃ vikalpanāt.
237.3

prayojanam anuddiśya na mando 'pi pravartate,
evam eva pravṛttiś cec caitanyenāsya kim bhavet.
653.5

pralaye 'pi pramāṇaṃ naḥ sarvacchedātmake na hi,
na ca prayojanaṃ tena syāt prajāpatikarmaṇā.
657.3

pravṛttiḥ katham ādyā ca jagataḥ saṃpratīyate,
śarīrāder vinā cāsya katham icchāpi sarjane.
651.3

prasiddhatvād ṛte sarvo vyavahāro hi neṣyate,
tasmād vedapramāṇārthaṃ nityatvam iha sādhyate.
730.1

prāyeṇaiva hi mīmāṃsā loke lokāyatīkṛtā,
tām āstikapathe kartum ayam yatnaḥ kṛto mayā.
4.1

buddhādīnām asārvajñyam iti satyaṃ vaco mama,
maduktatvād yathaivāgnir uṣṇo bhāsvara ity api.
85.2

buddhīnām api caitanyasvābhāvyāt puruṣasya naḥ,
nityatvam ekatā ceṣṭā bhedas tu viṣayāśrayaḥ.
833.5

bauddhadarśana ekasmin pakṣapāto na yujyate,
mṛṣātvaṃ yadi buddheḥ syād bādhaḥ kiṃ nopalabhyate.
237.7

bhārate 'pi bhaved evaṃ kartṛsmṛtyā tu bādhyate,
vede 'pi tatsmṛtir yā tu sārthavādanibandhanā.
949.3

bhāvātmake tathā meye nābhāvasya pramāṇatā,
tathābhāvaprameye 'pi na bhāvasya pramāṇatā.
489.3

bhinnasāmānyavacanā viśeṣavacanāś ca ye,
sarve bhaveyuḥ paryāyā yady apohasya vācyatā.
577.7

maṇḍūkavasayāktākṣā vaṃśān uragabuddhibhiḥ,
vyaktyalpatvamahattvābhyāṃ sāmānyaṃ ca tadāśrayam.
520.5

madhuraṃ tiktarūpeṇa śvetaṃ pītatayā tathā,
gṛhṇanti pittadoṣeṇa viṣayaṃ bhrāntacetasaḥ.
520.1

mānaṃ katham abhāvaś cet prameyaṃ cāsya kīdṛśam,
meyo yadvad abhāvo hi mānam apy evam iṣyatām.
489.1

mithyājñānaṃ na tatrāsti rāgadveṣādayo 'pivā,
manovṛttir hi sarveṣāṃ na cotpannaṃ tadā manaḥ.
664.3

mokṣārthī na pravarteta tatra kāmyaniṣiddhayoḥ,
nityanaimittike kuryāt pratyavāyajihāsayā.
671.5

yaḥ punar nānubhūto 'rtho na cāpy anubhaviṣyate,
vāsanābhāvatas tatra tavāpy anubhavaḥ katham.
326.3
yat kūpayūpasūpādau samāne 'py upabandhane,
nāsty arthānugamaḥ kaś cit tan na śabdo 'parādhyati.
91.1
yat tu brāhmaṇavastrādau brāhmaṇārtho na gamyate,
avadhyantaratas tatra tat padāntarajṛmbhitam.
907.3
yathā tantvādayaḥ siddhāḥ paramāṇuṣu satsv api,
tathā satsv api bhāgeṣu na varṇādi virotsyate.
888.5
yathā vā darpaṇaḥ svaccho yathā ca sphaṭiko 'malaḥ,
yad yan nidhīyate yogyaṃ tacchāyāṃ pratipadyate.
834.3
yathoṣṇe 'nuṣṇadhīr nāsti jñāne 'py ajñānadhīs tathā,
tena na jñānamātratve syād apohyaṃ kathaṃ cana.
308.1
yadi cāpauruṣeyy eṣā nānityapratipādinī,
pauruṣeyyās tu satyatvam katham adhyavasīyate.
954.3
yadi tv ādau jagat sṛṣṭvā dharmādharmau sasādhanau,
yathā śabdārthasaṃbandhān vedān kaś cit pravartayet.
650.2
yadi ca dhvanisaṃparkāc chrotram evopajāyate,
badhirasyāpi tajjanma kimarthaṃ nopalabhyate.
766.5
yadi (yadā) sarvam idaṃ nāsīt kvāvasthā tatra gamyatām,
prajāpateḥ kva vā sthānaṃ kiṃrūpaṃ ca pratīyatām.
650.6
yady api smṛtihetutvaṃ saṃskārasya vyavasthitam,
kāryāntareṣu sāmarthyaṃ na tasya pratiṣidhyate.
536.3

yad vā sarvagatatve 'pi vyaktiḥ śaktyanurodhataḥ,
śaktiḥ kāryānumeyā hi vyaktidarśanahetukā.
552.1

yasyānavayavaḥ sphoṭo vyajyate varṇabuddhibhiḥ,
so 'pi paryanuyogena naivaitena vimucyate.
533.4

yāvanto yādṛśā ye ca yadarthapratipādane,
varṇāḥ prajñātasāmarthyās te tathaivāvabodhakāḥ.
527.5

ye 'pi rekhādayo dṛṣṭā varṇānāṃ pratipādakāḥ,
na te svenāpi rūpeṇa paramārthatvavarjitāḥ.
256.4

yo 'dhunā paramārthena nāstīty evaṃ prakāśate,
kathaṃ pūrvam asāv āsīd asaṃś cet sādhanaṃ katham.
255.3

rucakādiṣu sāmānyaṃ rucakatvādy udāhṛtam,
bhinneṣu caiva sāmānyaṃ suvarṇatvaṃ pratīyate.
619.1

vaktur anyo hi saṃbandho buddhau śrotus tathāparaḥ,
śrotuḥ kartuṃ ca saṃbandhaṃ vaktā kaṃ pratipadya-
tām. 645.1

varṇātiriktaḥ pratiṣidhyamānaḥ
padeṣu mandaṃ phalam ādadhāti,
kāryāṇi vākyāvayavāśrayāṇi
satyāni kartuṃ kṛta eṣa yatnaḥ.
544.5

varṇāntaratvam evāhuḥ ke cid dīrghaplutādiṣu,
na hi drutādivat tatra prayogo nāntarīyakaḥ.
520.9

varṇā vā dhvanayo vāpi sphoṭaṃ na padavākyayoḥ,
vyañjanti vyañjakatvena yathā dīpaprabhādayaḥ.
542.11f.

varṇotthā vārthadhīr eṣā tajjñānānantarodbhavā,
yedṛśī sā tadutthā hi dhūmāder iva vahnidhīḥ.
544·1

vastvantarasya cābhāvāt tvayāpoho 'pi duṣkaraḥ,
nājñānaṃ nāma kiṃ cit syād apohyaṃ jñānavādinaḥ.
305·5

vahnir dahati nākāśaṃ ko 'tra paryanuyujyatām,
na cānyā mṛgyate yuktir yathā saṃdṛśyate tathā.
552·7

vākyārthamitaye teṣāṃ pravṛttau nāntarīyakam,
pāke jvāleva kāṣṭhānāṃ padārthapratipādanam.
943·3

vācyavācakasaṃbandhaniṣedhe lokabādhanam,
virodhaś ca svavākyena na hi saṃbandhavarjitaiḥ.
500·7

vāsanānugrahāt soktā kuṇapādimater iva,
bhāvanaiva ca vākyārthaḥ sarvatrākhyātavattayā.
939·1

vāsanābhedataś cet syāt prāptam anyonyasaṃśrayam,
svacchasya jñānarūpasya na hi bhedaḥ svato 'sti te.
260·9

vicchinnayatnavyaṅgyaiś ca nityaiḥ sarvagatair api,
vyatiriktapadārambho varṇair nātropapadyate.
526·5

vidyamānanimittaṃ ca kathyate nāsataḥ kriyā,
sādhāraṇaṃ ca tīrthādi kena cid vyapadiśyate.
953·5

vināpi vāsanātaś ced buddhir utpadyate tataḥ,
vāsanāyā nimittatvam abhyupetaṃ virudhyate.
326·5

vinā saṃskārakalpena tadanantaravṛttitaḥ,
kṛtānugrahasāmarthyo varṇo 'ntyaḥ pratipādakaḥ.
535·2

virodhitvena bādhyeta na tu madhvādibhakṣaṇam,
tasmād gurukule tiṣṭhan madhumāṃsādy avarjayan.
35.1

vedasyādhyayanaṃ sarvaṃ gurvadhyayana-pūrvakam,
vedādhyayanavācyatvād adhunādhyayanaṃ tathā.
949.1

vyatirikto hi saṃtāno yadi nābhyupagamyate,
saṃtāninām anityatvāt kartā kaś cin na labhyate.
697.9

vyavahārā hi dṛśyante sāmānyārthanibandhanāḥ,
dadhitakrādidānādau kauṇḍinyabrāhmaṇādiṣu.
617.9

śaktayaḥ sarvabhāvānāṃ bhāvaśabdair viśeṣataḥ,
nopākhyāyanta ity evaṃ nāpūrve dharmaśabdatā.
107.3

śaktayo 'pi ca bhāvānāṃ kāryārthāpattigocarāḥ,
prasiddhāḥ pāramārthikyaḥ pratikāryaṃ vyavasthitāḥ.
341.11

śabdānityatvapakṣe 'pi viśeṣeṇa sa duṣkaraḥ,
śabdaṃ tāvad anuccārya saṃbandhakaraṇaṃ kutaḥ.
795.1

śabdo 'pi pratyabhijñānāt prāg astīty avagamyate,
kūpapūraṇayatnena khaṃ tirodhīyate yadā.
737.9

śabdo vartata ity evaṃ tatra sarvātmakaś ca saḥ,
vyañjakadhvanyadhīnatvāt taddeśe tu sa gṛhyate.
773.3

śarīrendriyabuddhibhyo vyatiriktatvam ātmanaḥ,
nityatvaṃ ceṣyate śeṣam śarīrādi vinaśyati.
690.5

śreyaḥsādhanatā hy eṣāṃ nityaṃ vedāt pratīyate,
tādrūpyeṇa ca dharmatvaṃ tasmān nendriyagocaraḥ.
49.3

śreyo hi puruṣaprītiḥ sā dravyaguṇakarmabhiḥ,
codanālakṣaṇaiḥ sādhyā tasmāt teṣv eva dharmatā.
104.3

sa eveti matir nāpi sādṛśyaṃ na ca tat kva cit,
vināvayavasāmānyād varṇeṣv avayavā na ca.
514.7

saṃtāno 'yaṃ sa eveti na tv abhedād vinā bhavet,
vāyudīpādisaṃtāne vāyutvādir na bhidyate.
699.5

saṃbandhe gṛhyamāṇe ca saṃbandhigrahaṇaṃ bhavet,
tatrābhāvamatiḥ kena pramāṇenopalabhyate.
486.3

saṃvṛter na tu satyatvaṃ satyabhedaḥ kuto nv ayam,
satyaṃ cet saṃvṛtiḥ keyaṃ mṛṣā cet satyatā katham.
218.3

sadbhāve padavarṇānāṃ bhedo yaḥ paramāṇuvat,
sarvābhāvas tataś ceti seyaṃ bālabibhīṣikā.
888.3

sargapralayavijñānaṃ samastajagadāśrayam,
svaśarīravidāṃ puṃsāṃ nādhikenopayujyate.
672.3

sarvajñavan niṣedhyā ca sraṣṭuḥ sadbhāvakalpanā,
na ca dharmād ṛte tasya bhavel lokād viśiṣṭatā.
673.3

sarvatra na ca dhātvarthaḥ pratyayārthena yujyate,
bhāvanā pratyayārtho hi dhātvarthānāṃ ca tāṃ prati.
867.5

sarvatrālambanaṃ bāhyaṃ deśakālānyathātmakam,
janmany ekatra bhinne vā tathā kālāntare 'pi vā.
242.7.f

sarvathā kalpanāyāṃ ca cakṣuṣāpi rasādayaḥ,
gṛhyeran sarvabhāvānām aṇvākārāś ca tadgatāḥ.
281.3

sarvadā cāpi puruṣāḥ prāyeṇānṛtavādinaḥ,
yathādyatve na visrambhas tathātītārthakīrtane.
88.5

sarvavākyamṛṣātve tu dharmoktyaivātmabādhanam,
dharmyuktyāhaṃ yato jātaḥ sā vandhyā jananī mama.
366.4

sarveṇa śabdarūpaṃ ca vācakaṃ nityam iṣyate,
tatsvarūpe vivādas tu varṇās tatra ca sādhitāḥ.
820.2

sarveṣām anabhijñānāṃ pūrvapūrvaprasiddhitaḥ,
siddhaḥ saṃbandha ity evaṃ saṃbandhādir na vidyate.
649.5

sarveṣu caivam artheṣu mānasaṃ sarvavādinām,
iṣṭaṃ samuccayajñānaṃ kramajñāneṣu satsv api.
538.9

sādṛśyam atha sārūpyaṃ kasya keneti kathyatām,
na tāvac chābaleyena bāhuleyādayaḥ samāḥ.
563.5

sākṣād yady api kurvanti padārthapratipādanam,
varṇās tathāpi naitasmin paryavasyanti niṣphale.
943.1

sādhanaṃ cāsya dharmādi tadā kiṃ cin na vidyate,
na ca niḥsādhanaḥ kartā kaś cit sṛjati kiṃcana.
652.1

sādhanaṃ ced avaśyaṃ ca paramārthāstitā bhavet,
siddhir nāparamārthena paramārthasya yujyate.
255.5

sāsnādibhyas tu piṇḍasya bhedo nātyantato yadā,
sāmānyasya ca piṇḍebhyas tadā syād etad uttaram.
557.3

sā hi syāc chabdasaṃskārād indriyasyobhayasya vā,
tatra sarvaiḥ pratīyeta śabdaḥ saṃskriyate yadi.
744.1

sukhaduḥkhādyavasthāś ca gacchann api naro mama,
caitanyadravyasattādirūpaṃ naiva vimuñcati.
695.3

sukhopabhogarūpaś ca yadi mokṣaḥ prakalpyate,
svarga eva bhaved eṣa paryāyeṇa kṣayī ca saḥ.
670.1

svataḥ sarvapramāṇānāṃ prāmāṇyam iti gamyatām,
na hi svato 'satī śaktiḥ kartum anyena śakyate.
59.3

svato hrasvādibhedas tu nityavāde virudhyate,
sarvadā yasya sadbhāvaḥ sa kathaṃ mātrikaḥ svayam.
522.1

svarūpeṇa yathā vahnir nityaṃ dahanakarmakaḥ,
upanītaṃ dahaty arthaṃ dāhyaṃ nānyan na cānyathā.
834.1

svayaṃ ca śuddharūpatvād asattvāc cānyavastunaḥ,
svapnādivad avidyāyāḥ pravṛttis tasya kiṃkṛtā.
663.1

svādhīnatvāc ca dharmādes tena kleśo na yujyate,
tadvaśena pravṛttau vā vyatirekaḥ prasajyate.
662.5

hetuṣv evaṃ parokteṣu pratiṣiddheṣu saṃprati,
ahaṃpratyayavijñeyaḥ svayam ātmopapadyate.
716.3

hyastanoccāritas tasmād gośabdo 'dyāpi vidyate,
gośabdajñānagamyatvād yathokto 'dyaiṣa gaur iti.
837.3

—::—

FROM THE TANTRAVĀRTTIKA

One hundred and ninety four *kārikās* have been selected from the *Tantravārttika,* most of which have been cited by different authors in their compositions. For page references please consult the *Tantravārttika,* A Gloss on Śabaraswāmin's Commentary on the *Mīmāṃsā Sūtras* by Bhaṭṭa Kumārila, ed. by Paṇḍit Dhuṇḍhirāja Panta, Benares Sanskrit Series No. 5. Fasciculus I. Benares 1882 and the Work with the same name, Benares Sanskrit Series Nos. 5, 7, 16, 23, 27, 29, 32, 34, 36, 39, 60, 62, & 72, ed. by Mahāmahopādhyāya Paṇḍit Gaṅgādhara Śāstrī C.I.E. Benares, 1903.

atra cākṛtir eveti dṛḍhaḥ pakṣo 'yam ekataḥ,
itare tv anyataḥ sarve vyaktipakṣānuyāyinaḥ.
247.19

athavā naiva bhidyete yāgahomau parasparam,
pūrvāparau hi sadṛśau tadbhāgau narasiṃhavat.
1030.1

anūdya cāpi dhātvarthaṃ guṇaḥ sarvo vidhīyate,
na cānuvādaḥ prakṛtāt karmaṇo 'nyatra labhyate.
296.20

anyataḥ siddhaśeṣāṇāṃ yeṣāṃ dṛṣṭopakāritā,
teṣāṃ nāpūrvam astīti hantyādīnām udāhṛtiḥ.
386.12

anyatra jñātasadbhāvaḥ padārtho 'nyatra vāryate,
na tv ekatraiva sadrūpam asadrūpaṃ ca gamyate.
323.16

anyad eva hi yāgādau sāmānyaṃ karaṇātmakam,
anyac ca bhāvanā nāma sādhyatvena vyavasthitam.
351.20

anyad eva hi dhātvarthaprāpyaṃ karma sakarmake
anyad eva ca sarvatra pratyayārthanibandhanam.
354.24f.

anyonyanirapekṣāṇāṃ kāryānyatve niyogataḥ,
pratyekaṃ yāgahetutvād yajuṣṭvam avakalpate.
433.2

apūrvo vaiṣa codyeta bhakṣaḥ prakṛta eva vā,
saṃskāro 'rthakriyā vā syāt saṃskāro yāgasādhanam.
1063.20

apoddhāreṇa saṃskāro yady atrābhyupagamyate,
śṛṅgaṃ śaśād apoddhṛtya kiṃ na saṁskriyate manāk.
220.3

abhidhābhāvanām āhur anyām eva liṅādayaḥ,
arthātmabhāvanā tv anyā sarvākhyāteṣu gamyate.
344.24f.

abhidheyāvinābhūte pravṛttir lakṣaṇeṣyate,
lakṣyamāṇaguṇair yogād vṛtter iṣṭā tu gauṇatā.
318.6

artho 'pi yādṛśo yatra devatātvena coditaḥ,
manāg api tato 'nyatve devateti na gamyate.
402.16

astyādāv api kartraṃśe bhāvye 'sty eva hi bhāvanā,
anyatrāśeṣabhāvāt tu na tathā sā prakāśate.
349.1

ākāṅkṣā saṃnidhānaṃ ca yogyatā ceti ca trayam,
saṃbandhakāraṇatvena kḷptaṃ nānantaraśrutiḥ.
438.20

ākāśe 'vasthitāḥ śabdāḥ saṃskartuṃ śakyate katham,
nityatvān mūrtyabhāvāc ca vyomāśritavibhutvavat.
218.21

ākhyātavartī dhātvarthaḥ sādhyarūpaḥ pratīyate,
tasmin phalavatīṣṭe tu nāmno dṛṣṭārthateṣyate.
359.2

āyurvedam cikitsāsu prāyeṇa viniyujyate, (sic.)
vyādhitattvauṣadhijñānaṃ vaidyebhyaś copalabhyate.
204.23

āryās tāvad viśiṣyerann adṛṣṭārtheṣu karmasu,
dṛṣṭārtheṣu tu tulyatvam āryamlecchaprayoginām.
149.2

āvirbhūtaikayā śaktyā dravyam ātmavaśīkṛtam,
na śaktyantarayogitvaṃ tadaiva pratipatsyate.
967.23

udgātā gauṇa evātra mukhyodgātur asaṃbhavāt,
kalpito 'yaṃ parāvṛttyā brāhmaṇādiṣu rājavat.
1049.2

udgātṛpadam audgātraṃ prasūte taddhite kṛte,
na tv audgātṛpadād asya vyutpattir upapadyate.
1048.20

ṛtvigbhyo dakṣiṇāṃ dadyād iti dānaṃ vidhīyate,
lobhād evārjanāṅgatvāt prāptas teṣāṃ parigrahaḥ.
999.5

ṛṣayo 'pi hi lakṣyāṇāṃ nāntaṃ yānti pṛthaktvaśaḥ,
lakṣaṇena tu siddhānām antaṃ yānti vipaścitaḥ.
416.6

ekakālaprayoge hi virodho mantrayor bhavet,
karaṇaḥ prāk kriyātas tu parataś cetaraḥ sthitaḥ.
1171.13

ekakālābhisaṃyogād bhinnānām api karmaṇām,
samudāyārpaṇaṃ śakyam ekadeśasthavṛkṣavat.
468.19

ekārthatvaṃ padasya syāt sākāṅkṣāvayavaṃ na tat,
sākāṅkṣāvayavaḥ saṃghas tasyaiko 'rtho na vidyate.
428.12

eko rogo hato yasya yasya vāpahṛtā daśa,
arogitve tayor bhedo na kaś cid api vidyate.
370.2

karotiḥ kriyamāṇena na kaś cit karmaṇā vinā,
bhavatyarthasya kartā ca karoteḥ karma jāyate.
343.2

karmaṇo bheda evāyaṃ vākyabhedo 'bhidhīyate,
saṃbandhety ekavākyatvam arthānyatve 'pi gamyate.
1099.24

kalpanād dhi prayogāṇāṃ kalpo 'nuṣṭhānasādhanam,
sūtraṃ tu sūcanāt teṣāṃ svayaṃ kalpyaprayojakam.
161.16

kasya cij jāyate tuṣṭir aśubhe 'pi hi karmaṇi,
śākyasyeva kuhetūktir vedabrāhmaṇadūṣaṇe.
129.4

kāmaṃ vā so 'rthavādo 'stu sāmānyastho ghṛte vidhiḥ,
vinā stutyā vidhānaṃ tu snehadravyāntare bhavet.
330.24 f.

kutaḥ kṛtārthasaṃyoge deśakālopalakṣaṇam,
sarveṣv iṣṭaṃ kṛtārthau ca vediyūpāv ihānyataḥ.
1135.14

kṛtaḥ kaṭa itīhāpi karmatvaṃ niṣṭhayocyate,
tasminn abhihite saṃkhyā na dvitīyaṃ grahīṣyate.
974.5

kratvaṅgatvena naiveha sadasyasya nirākriyā,
camasādhvaryuvat tv eṣa na ṛtvig ity abhidhīyate.
1150.5

kriyayā kārakaṃ gamyaṃ kārakeṇa kriyā tathā,
ekasyāpy anapekṣatve na mūlam avadhāritam.
961.3

krītarājakabhojyānnavākyaṃ cātharvavaidikam,
na ca tasyāpramāṇatve kiṃ cid apy asti kāraṇam.
107.20

guṇāntarāvaruddhatvān nāvakāśo guṇo 'paraḥ,
vikalpo 'pi na vaiṣamyāt tasmān nāmaiva yujyate.
309.7

guṇārthaupavasathye 'hni savanīyapunaḥśrutiḥ,
utpattiḥ prakriyā caiṣām āśvinagrahaṇottarā.
1092.15

guṇo vā nāmadheyaṃ vā samidādipadaṃ bhavet,
tābhyām eva ca bhedo 'tra kim abhyāsaḥ kariṣyati.
450.4

gauṇo vā yadi mukhyo vā vedān āśrīyate hi yaḥ,
sa dharmasādhanatvena padārtho 'dhyavasīyate.
154.1

caturvidhe pade cātra dvividhasyārthanirṇayaḥ,
kriyate saṃśayotpatter nopasarganipātayoḥ.
260.23f.

coditaṃ hy upadiṣṭaṃ vā prayuktaṃ vā kriyāgatam,
mlecchair avadhṛtaṃ paścād āryair dvaibhāṣikaiḥ kva cit.
158.9

jātir vyaktiś ca saṃbandhaḥ samūho liṅgakārake,
saṃkhyā ca saptamī teṣām aṣṭapakṣī dvayor dvayoḥ.
267.9

tathā kramavator nityaṃ prakṛtipratyayāṃśayoḥ,
pratyayaśrutivelāyāṃ bhāvanātmāvagamyate.
348.15

tathātikrāntavedoktamaryādāvyavahāriṇām,
saṃvādiṣv api vākyeṣu neṣyate dharmahetutā.
126.23

tathāyaṃ caruśabdo 'pi loke sthālīnibandhanaḥ,
yājñikānāṃ ca vede ca prasiddhas tv odanaṃ prati.
152.11

tathaikadhātusaṃbaddhabhāvanācodane sati,
bhāvanāntaragāminyaḥ syur dhātvantaracodanāḥ.
448.19

tayor arthābhidhāne hi vyāpāro naiva vidyate,
yadarthadyotakau tau tu vācakaḥ sa vicāryate.
261.2

tasmāt padeṣu yāvatsu śrūyamāṇeṣu dṛśyate,
viśiṣṭam aikyam arthasya tāvatām ekavākyatā.
426.17

tasmād yāny eva śāstrāṇi vedamūlānatikramāt,
avasthitāni tair eva jñāto dharmaḥ phalapradaḥ.
126.19

tasmān mlecchaprasiddhaṃ yat padam āryair vikalpyate,
na kaś cit tatra viśvāso yuktaḥ padapadārthayoḥ.
157.21

tān eva vaidikān varṇān bhāratādiniveśitān,
svādhyāyaniyamaṃ hitvā lokabuddhyā prayuñjate.
436.1

tulyo 'bhidhānapakṣe 'pi sa doṣaḥ śabdagocaraḥ,
vācakasyāpy anekānto gamakasyeva neṣyate.
975.10

te ca sarve 'bhidhīyante vyāmohavinivṛttaye,
gaur ity uccarite sapta vastūni pratibhānti naḥ.
267.7

tena bhūtiṣu kartṛtvaṃ pratipannasya vastunaḥ,
prayojakakriyām āhur bhāvanāṃ bhāvanāvidaḥ.
344.20

tena vedaviruddhānāṃ smṛtīnām apramāṇatā,
ruddhaśrutyanumānatvād anyamūlā hi tā yataḥ.
89.12

dharmo 'pi hi vṛṇoty eva naraṃ saṃsāravartinam,
na hi kevalapāpena dehenācchidyate naraḥ.
1002.12

na karmāntaratāsty atra balavatpratyabhijñayā,
na copātto guṇaḥ kaś cin na ca vākyāntare śrutiḥ.
412.10

na ca vedāṅgabhāvo 'pi kaś cid vyākaraṇaṃ prati,
tādarthyāvayavābhāvād buddhādivacaneṣv iva.
207.21

na ca śīghrahṛte 'rthe 'sti cirād āgacchato gatiḥ,
aśvair apahṛtaṃ ko hi gardabhaiḥ prāptum arhati.
92.8

na cāvaśyaṃ pradānena havir āgneyam iṣyate,
dvyavadāne gṛhīte hi sarvāgneyatvasaṃbhavaḥ.
1019.18

na tāvad anṛṣiḥ kaś cit smaryate kalpasūtrakṛt,
kartṛtvaṃ yad ṛṣīṇāṃ tu tat sarvaṃ mantrakṛtsamam.
164.1

na mukhyātikrame kiṃ cid dṛśyate kāraṇāntaram,
mukhyatvasya vivakṣā tu yatheṣṭaṃ na na yujyate.
972.23

na hy eṣa karmasaṃskāro hūyamānasya veṣyate,
hutaśeṣasamānatvāt tantratvaṃ tu pratīyate.
1043.2

nānyatrotsahate gantuṃ vaidikaṃ saṃnibandhanam,
yatheṣṭaviniyogaṃ tu sarvārthaṃ vastu laukikam.
435.16

nāmākhyātārthasaṃbandhe yad akḷptaprayojanam,
tasyādṛṣṭārthatā yuktā netarasyāpramāṇikā.
383.12

nityaṃ na bharaṇaṃ yasya yasya vā nityabhūtatā,
na tasya kriyamāṇatvaṃ khapuṣpākāśayor iva.
343.10

nirvapann eva jānāti hy etāvad iha dāsyate,
tatrādhikaparityāgaḥ kalpyate kena hetunā.
1023.7

nyūnavākyaprayogo hi vede naiva samāśritaḥ,
kaś cit kvāpi sthitaḥ śeṣaḥ so 'nveṣṭavyaḥ prayatnataḥ.
435.3

patrorṇavāravāṇādi yac ca taddeśasaṃbhavam,
tair evākathitaṃ nāma tac ca ko vedituṃ kṣamaḥ.
160.6

padam ajñātasaṃbandhaṃ prasiddhair apṛthakśruti,
nirṇīyate nirūḍhaṃ tu na svārthād apanīyate.
286.1

padārthaiḥ padavijñātair vākyārthaḥ pratipadyate,
lokasiddhair na tatrāsti vākyaikatvanimittatā.
426.22

paratrāviṅayaṃ kurvan pitṛbhyāṃ vāryate sutaḥ,
tayor evāvinītasya ko bhaved vinivārakaḥ.
237.1

parastād arthavādeṣu svatantro jāyate hy asau,
purastād arthavādeṣu tatpūrvā vidhikalpanā.
1006.17

parikrayo hi sarvatra svena dravyeṇa kalpate,
devatārthe parityakte svāmitvaṃ na ca kasya cit.
1032.22

puruṣasya sacailasya snānaṃ yasmād vidhīyate,
tasmāt puruṣavad vastraṃ na gavāśvādivan matam.
99.22

puruṣārthasamāsatteḥ kāmyaṃ nityasya bādhakam,
viśeṣataś ca sāmānye pūrvatrāpte pravartanāt.
316.2

puruṣārtho hi sarveṇa svarasād eva kāmyate,
tatsādhanatadaṅgeṣu pravṛttiḥ prārthanād ṛte.
292.15

paurṇamāsīsamidyāgād āmāvasyo na bhidyate,
yajamānāntareṣv evaṃ deśabhedeṣv avasthitam.
456.4

pratipādyam idaṃ dravyaṃ bhedena sahate kriyām,
khaṇḍaśaś ca pradhānānām aṅgatvān nāsti tantratā.
1042.11

pratyakṣapratyabhijñānāc chabdaikatvaṃ pratiṣṭhitam,
ekaśabdotthitajñānagrāhyatvāc caikavākyatā.
244.21

pratyayārthaṃ saha brūtaḥ prakṛtipratyayau sadā,
prādhānyād bhāvanā tena pratyayārtho ’vadhāryate.
348.11

pratyayārthaḥ samāno ’pi dhātubhedena bhidyate,
dhātor api samānatve kena bhedo ’vadhāryate.
451.18

prathamaṃ hi svavākyasthair guṇaiḥ saṃbadhyate kriyā,
vākyāntaragataiḥ paścān na śuddhā sā hy avāpyate.
292.5

pradhānaupayikaṃ dravyam saṃskārair api yujyate,
tena hantyādibhiḥ sarvaiḥ saṃskartavyāḥ priyaṅgavaḥ.
384.17

pradhānaṃ nīyamānaṃ hi tatrāṅgāny api karṣati,
aṅgam ākṛṣyamāṇaṃ tu nāṅgāntaram asaṃgateḥ.
477.18

pravaro na tv atikrānto yājyākāle 'panīyate,
bhakṣaṇasya tu bhāvitvāc chaktyāpanayakalpanā.
1060.1

pravartanasmṛtiḥ prāpte praiṣa ity abhidhīyate,
aprāptapraiṣaṇaṃ sarvaṃ vidhitvaṃ pratipadyate.
351.5

prāpte karmaṇi nāneko vidhātuṃ śakyate guṇaḥ,
aprāpte tu vidhīyante bahavo 'py ekayatnataḥ.
476.6

prāsaṅgikīṃ kratoḥ siddhiṃ kāmyo hi kurute guṇaḥ,
gṛhṇanti na ca siddhārthāḥ kratavaḥ svaguṇaṃ tadā.
1082.24

priyaṅgavaḥ śaratpakvās tāvad gacchanti hi kṣayam,
yadā varṣāsu modante samyag jātāḥ priyaṅgavaḥ.
148.2

phalavākye yajer eva saṃbandhaḥ śrūyate sphuṭaḥ,
tatsaṃnidhau samāmnānāj juhoter aṅgateṣyate.
1028.11

phalena yasya saṃbandhas tato 'pūrvaṃ prakalpyate,
tadalpatvopapattau ca na yuktā bahukalpanā.
339.11

phālgune 'nyauṣadhīnāṃ tu jāyate patraśātanam,
modamānās tu tiṣṭhanti yavāḥ kaṇiśaśālinaḥ.
147.24f.

balavantaṃ parityajya yaḥ pratiṣṭhātum icchati,
hastinā pādayodhīva saṃtiṣṭhetācirād asau.
103.4

bhāvanaiva ca vākyārthaḥ svakārakaviśeṣitā,
tasyāś ca jñāyate nityaṃ bhedaḥ śabdāntarādibhiḥ.
427.7

bhāvārthāḥ karmaśabdā ye tebhyo 'pūrvakriyāgatiḥ,
taiḥ kuryād yajinā svargaṃ eṣa hy artho vidhīyate.
341.6

bhūtabhāvyupayogaṃ hi saṃskāryaṃ dravyam iṣyate,
saktavo nopayokṣyante nopayuktāś ca te kva cit.
389.4

bhrātṝṇām ekajātānām ekaś cet putravān bhavet,
sarve tenaiva putreṇa putriṇo manur abravīt.
135.2

bhrānter anubhavād vāpi puṃvākyād vipralambhanāt,
dṛṣṭānuguṇyasādhyatvāc codanaiva laghīyasī.
74.12

mīmāṃsā cāpi vedārthatattvanirṇayakāraṇam,
vyapadeśādibhedaiś ca na bhedo 'trānumīyate.
266.11

yajñāṅgatvāc ca taccheṣāḥ pradhānenaikakartṛkāḥ,
pradhānasya ca yaḥ kartā svāmī dātā sa vājinām.
1004.10

yatra deśe hi yaḥ śabdo yasminn arthe prayujyate,
śaktis tadgocarā tasya vācakākhyā pramīyate.
146.4

yatra varṇavikāro vā varṇalopo 'pi vā smṛtaḥ,
svarāntaraniyogo vā na mantras tatra neṣyate.
418.12

yatrārthasya visaṃvādaḥ pratyakṣeṇopalabhyate,
svarasaṃskāramātrārthā tatra vyākaraṇasmṛtiḥ.
399.18

yathā kāṣṭhatṛṇādīnāṃ mārutād eva śuddhatā,
smaryate vāsaso naivaṃ toyaprakṣālanād vinā.
99.12

yathā ca padmarāgādīn kācasphaṭikamiśritān,
parīkṣakā vijānanti sādhutvam apare tathā.
232.7

yathā raktopadhānena niruddhe sphaṭike sati,
kṛṣṇādicodanāyuktaṃ gamyate sphaṭikāntaram.
448.17

yathā ratnaparīkṣāyāṃ sādhvasādhutvalakṣaṇam,
tathā vyākaraṇāt siddhaṃ sādhuśabdanirūpaṇam.
232.9

yathā sādhvanurūpatvāt pramādāśaktijeṣv api,
jāyate vācakabhrāntis tathaiva mlecchabhāṣite.
149.18

yathaiva lokasiddhatvāt kṛṣyāder lakṣaṇaṃ vṛthā,
tathaiva vedasiddhānāṃ śabdānāṃ lakṣaṇaṃ vṛthā.
203.21

yathaivānyāyavijñātād vedāl lekhyādipūrvakāt,
śūdreṇādhigatād vāpi dharmajñānaṃ na saṃmatam.
126.21

yathaivāśrāddhabhojitvaṃ yathā vā māṃsabhakṣaṇam,
śreyase vihitaṃ dharmyaṃ na sarvatra niṣidhyate.
111.3

yadi ca dravyavācitvaṃ suptiṅanteṣv apīṣyate,
tato liṅgādiyogaḥ syāt sattvabhāvāt kṛdantavat.
967.15

yadi tv anyanivṛttyaiva pariśeṣaḥ prakalpyate,
śaśaśṛṅganimittatvaṃ phalānāṃ kiṃ na gamyate.
361.20

yad eva bhavatāṃ gotraṃ tad asmākam apītivat,
āhuḥ svāgamanityatvaṃ paravākyānukāriṇaḥ.
170.1

yad vā karmavināśo 'yaṃ phalaṃ naḥ sādhayiṣyati,
aṅgiyāgavidhānād dhi tad ayatnena kalpyate.
362.17

yamādayo na vidyante yady api grahadevatāḥ,
anyakarmopayogitvāt prakāśyāḥ syus tathāpi naḥ.
407.11

yāgadānādyanusyūto bhāvanātmāvagamyate,
nityam ākhyātaśabdebhyas tasmād bhāvārthateṣyate.
340.20

yāgasādhanatāṃ kuryāt pūtikānāṃ yadi śrutiḥ,
tataḥ syāt kāryavartitvaṃ na tv evaṃ sā pravartate.
1107.9

yāgād eva phalaṃ tad dhi śaktidvāreṇa sidhyati,
sūkṣmaśaktyātmakaṃ vā tat phalam evopajāyate.
367.22

yā coktā pāṇḍuputrāṇām ekapatnīviruddhatā,
sāpi dvaipāyanenaiva vyutpādya pratipāditā.
135.15

yā tu vedaviruddheha smṛtiḥ kācana dṛśyate,
sā tu syād bhrāntimūlaiva na spaṣṭaśrutimūlatā.
86.24f.

yādṛśī bhāvanākhyāte dhātvarthaś cāpi yādṛśaḥ,
nāsau tenaiva rūpeṇa kathyate 'nyaiḥ padaiḥ kva cit.
352.6

yāvan na vidhisaṃsparśas tāvan nāsya prayojanam,
vinā ca tena dhātvartho na kratvaṅgaṃ pratīyate.
976.4

yā vedabāhyāḥ smṛtayo yāś ca kāś cit kudṛṣṭayaḥ,
sarvās tā niṣphalāḥ pretya tamoniṣṭhā hi tāḥ smṛtāḥ.
117.20

yenaiva hetunaiteṣāṃ svāmigāmitvaniścayaḥ,
tenaiva tu pradhānārthapratipattir api sphuṭā.
1130.15

yeṣāṃ darśanamātre 'pi veda eva na paṭhyate,
saṃbhāṣāpi ca na mlecchaiḥ sahāryāvartavāsinām.
156.9

yogyatā liṅgam ity uktaṃ tac ceṣṭaṃ viniyojakam,
bhakṣayogyaḥ puroḍāśaḥ svarūpeṇa ca dṛśyate.
1033.7

lakāre lakṣaṇā tāvad ādeśārthaṃ prasajyate,
sthānidvārā parokṣā ca vṛttir ādeśabhāg bhavet.
976.12

lokaḥ smarati taṃ mantraṃ viṣāpaharaṇādiṣu,
yathā vā sarpasiddhānte nakulo yāṃ kilauṣadhim.
133.9

lokād evādhigantavyā śabdānāṃ sādhvasādhutā,
vācakāvācakatvena sā ca nityaṃ vyavasthitā.
190.19

lokāyatikamūrkhāṇāṃ naivānyat karma vidyate,
yāvat kiṃ cid adṛṣṭārthaṃ tad dṛṣṭārthaṃ hi kurvate.
85.13

loke tu sarvabhāṣābhir arthā vyākaraṇād ṛte,
sidhyanti vyavahāreṇa kāvyādiṣv apy asaṃśayam.
205.9

loko yad anyataḥ siddhaṃ nābhidheyaṃ tad icchati,
yathā śrotṛgṛhītatvāt svarūpaṃ nābhidhīyate.
966.17

laukikāśrayaṇaṃ tatra yatra nānyo 'sti vaidikaḥ,
vaidike dakṣiṇādāne sati kiṃ laukikāśrayaḥ.
1160.12

laukike 'pi tu yo dātā śūdrādir na sa doṣavān,
pratigrahītṛdoṣas tu punar apy ubhayoḥ samaḥ.
997.26

vākyasphoṭaś ca yair iṣṭaḥ sarvāvayavavarjitaḥ,
nāmākhyātādi saṃskāryaṃ teṣāṃ śaśaviṣāṇavat.
220.1

vākyārtheṣu ca saṃdehā jāyante ye sahasraśaḥ,
naiṣāṃ vyākaraṇāt kaś cit pūrvapakṣo 'pi gamyate.
211.11

vidyamāneṣu śeṣeṣu dravyāṇām aprayojakāḥ,
bhaveyuḥ śeṣabhājo hi niḥśeṣe tu prayojakāḥ.
1015.21

vidhāne cānuvāde ca yāgaḥ karaṇam iṣyate,
tatsamīpe tṛtīyāntas tadvācitvaṃ na muñcati.
284.22

vidheyebhyo yathāpūrvaṃ vidhiśāstreṣu gamyate,
tathaiva pratiṣedhebhyaḥ pratiṣedhais tad ucyate.
376.15

vibhaktayo vidhīyante yatra tasya viśeṣaṇam,
yujyate 'nabhidhānaṃ hi na punas tadviśeṣaṇe.
973.8

virodhe tv anapekṣaṃ syāt prāmāṇyaṃ smṛtibandhanam,
avirodhe hi vedena tanmūlam anumīyate.
86.22

viśeṣavihitaṃ tv etat prāpte cānavakāśakam,
puruṣārthasamīpe ca camasaṃ tena bādhate.
1083.23

viṣayāviṣayau jñātvā tenotsargāpavādayoḥ,
bādhābādhau vivektavyau na tu sāmānyadarśanāt.
88.18

vedatvaṃ kalpasūtrāṇāṃ na moktavyaṃ manāg api,
yadi vā vedatulyatvaṃ svatantrāṇāṃ pratīyatām.
163.13

vedād ṛte, 'pi kurvanti kalpaiḥ karmāṇi yājñikāḥ,
na tu kalpair vinā ke cin mantrabrāhmaṇamātrakāt.
165.19

vede vyākaraṇādīni santy evābhyantarāṇi naḥ,
bhaved vā tadabhiprāyā ṣaḍaṅgādhyayanasmṛtiḥ.
208.17

vyaktir vācyeti vijñānaṃ na sanmūlam asaṃbhavāt,
tena vyākaraṇe 'pīdṛg na pramāṇaṃ smṛtir matā.
262.14

vyaktau nirākṛtāyāṃ ca samastānāṃ nirākriyā,
sulabheti na sarve 'mī bhāṣyakāreṇa darśitāḥ.
247.21

śaktayaḥ sarvabhāvāṇāṃ nānuyojyāḥ svabhāvataḥ,
tena nānā vadanty arthān prakṛtipratyayādayaḥ.
344.17

śaktibhiḥ sarvabhāvānāṃ vyavahārānupātitā,
tenānyadeśakāle 'pi rūpe tābhiḥ sa sidhyati.
367.9

śatabrāhmaṇasaṃyukto vidhir atrāvagamyate,
anyathā tadupādānaṃ gauṇaṃ vyarthaṃ ca te bhavet.
1067.6

śākyādayaś ca sarvatra kurvāṇā dharmadeśanām,
hetujālavinirmuktāṃ na kadācana kurvate.
117.13

śāstreṇa coditā ye hi darvihomāḥ svarūpataḥ,
teṣv evāhavanīyaḥ syān na yāgeṣv apy acodanāt.
1152.14

śiṣyānuśāsanatvaṃ hi śāstrāṇām upapadyate,
śabdasyānanuśāsyatvād vyarthaṃ tadanuśāsanam.
219.21

śūdrānnabhojanenāpi tuṣyanty anye dvijātayaḥ,
svamātulasutāṃ prāpya dākṣiṇātyas tu tuṣyati.
129.10

śeṣaśeṣyādayaḥ sarve karmabhedanibandhanāḥ,
kārye jñāte 'dhikāraḥ syād upadeśe 'tideśadhīḥ.
337.2

śrutiliṅge yathā ceṣṭe vyavasthitabalābale,
saṃnikṛṣṭavikṛṣṭārthe tathaiveha śrutismṛtī.
92.14

śrutyā hi devatā yāge samavaiti na rūpataḥ,
tasmān māhendraśabdoktyā mahendro devateṣyate.
402.10

śrūyate doṣasaṃyuktaḥ sa ca doṣo 'sti laukike,
vaidike vidhigamyatvān na hi doṣaḥ prasajyate.
996.11

śrūyamāṇasya vākyasya nyūnādhikavikalpane,
lakṣaṇāvākyabhedādidoṣo nānumite hy asau.
201.4

śrautavyāpāranānātve śabdānām atigauravam,
ekoktyavasitānāṃ tu nārthākṣepo virudhyate.
476.22

saṃkhyāyāṃ kārake vā dhīr vibhaktyā hi pravartate,
ubhayaṃ cātra tat siddhaṃ bhāvanātiṅvibhaktitaḥ.
970.10

saṃnikṛṣṭo na labdhaś ced viprakṛṣṭo 'pi vaidikaḥ,
sa evāvaidikas tu syāt prāptaḥ saṃnihito yadā.
437.2

saṃbandhamātram uktaṃ ca śrutyā dhātvarthabhā-
vayoḥ,
tadekāṃśaniveśe tu vyāpāro 'syā na vidyate.
353.6

saṃsargo 'pi padārthānām anyonyenānurañjanam,
ekaikatra tad apy astīty ekatvaṃ na pratīyate.
429.11

samāpyate vidhiḥ kaś cit kadā cin nāprarocitaḥ,
ghṛte prarocanāṃ dṛṣṭvā vidhis tatrānumīyate.
331.7

samudāyārthavācitve naikadeśe bhaved gatiḥ,
śataśabdān na pañcāśan mukhyarūpeṇa gamyate.
319.20

sarvatrākhyātasaṃbaddhe śrūyamāṇe padāntare,
vidhiśaktyupasaṃkrānte syād dhātor anuvādatā.
290.1

sarvatraiva hi vijñānaṃ saṃskāratvena gamyate,
parāṅgaṃ cātmavijñānād anyatrety avadhāraṇāt.
240.15

sarvāśramātiriktena svādhyāyenaiva śodhitaḥ,
stokair apy āśramācārair gatim iṣṭāṃ gamiṣyati.
113.1

savanīyān purotpādya vapām utkṛṣya vākyataḥ,
tatrāpy aniyame prāpte tadviśeṣo vidhīyate.
1093.24

sākṣād avyabhicāreṇa dhātvartho yatra karmabhāk,
sakarmakaḥ sa dhātuḥ syāt pāramparye tv akarmakaḥ.
355.19

sādhyasādhanasaṃbandhaḥ sarvadā bhāvanāśrayaḥ,
tena tasya na siddhiḥ syād bhāvanāpratyayād ṛte.
357.9

sādhyātmako 'pi dhātvartho yadā nāmnābhidhīyate,
tadā dravyavad evāsau niṣpannātmā pratīyate.
359.10

sādhyāṃśe puruṣāṇāṃ ca pratyayo na niyojakaḥ,
svayam eva hi jānanti kartavyaṃ puruṣāḥ sadā.
353.12

sāmarthyaṃ karmaṇas tāvad ekaṃ liṅgaṃ vivakṣitam,
aparaṃ vākyasāmarthyaṃ paurvāparyanirīkṣaṇāt.
1005.17

sāmarthyaṃ sarvabhāvānām arthāpattyāvagamyate,
ekasāmarthyasiddhe 'rthe nānekaṃ tac ca labhyate.
225.17

sāmānyavidhir aspaṣṭaḥ saṃhriyeta viśeṣataḥ,
spaṣṭasya tu vidher nānyair upasaṃhārasaṃbhavaḥ.
1020.11

siddhakartṛkriyāvāciny ākhyātapratyaye sati,
sāmānādhikaraṇyena karotyartho 'vagamyate.
342.7

siddharūpaḥ prayogo yaiḥ karmaṇām anugamyate,
te kalpā lakṣaṇārthāni sūtrāṇīti pracakṣate.
161.14

siddho lokapravādo 'yam ekānekavināśinām,
sarvanāśe samutpanne hy ardhaṃ tyajati paṇḍitaḥ.
91.7

sukhaduḥkhātmakatvena samāneṣv eva janmasu,
kriyānantaram eveha staḥ svarganarakāv api.
364.3

sūtravārttikabhāṣyeṣu dṛśyate cāpaśabdanam,
aśvārūḍhāḥ kathaṃ cāśvān vismareyuḥ sacetanāḥ.
201.3

stutīnāṃ vidhyadhīnatvād anuvādāc ca lakṣaṇā,
mukhyatvāt tu vidher nāsāv avirodhāc ca kalpyate.
330.13

stuter aparimāṇatvād yāvatī hi pratīyate,
tāṃ sarvām aikarūpyeṇa vidhyuddeśaḥ pratīcchati.
315.11

sthālyāder yo 'pi kartṛtvaṃ tadānīm adhyavasyati,
nādhārād anyathābhūtaṃ vyāpārāṃ so 'pi vindati.
971.9

svaravarṇānupūrvyādiviśiṣṭe hi prayujyate,
mantraśabdas tato 'nyatve na tasyārthaḥ pratīyate.
417.16

svāṅgena pāñcadaśyena vyāptās tā hy atideśataḥ,
vihitaṃ sāmadhenyaṅgaṃ sāptadaśyaṃ na gṛhṇate.
1078.7

svārthabodhe samāptānām aṅgāṅgitvādyapekṣayā,
vākyānām ekavākyatvaṃ punaḥ saṃhatya jāyate.
329.24f.

— : : —

WITTY REMARKS OF KUMĀRILA BHAṬṬA

Some of the witty remarks made by Kumārila Bhaṭṭa have been collected from the selected *kārikās* given in the foregoing pages and are presented below :

asatā yat tu sādṛśyam asataḥ parikalpyate,
dhruvaṃ śaśaviṣāṇena kharaśṛṅgasya tad bhavet.
(p. 36)

A comparison, which is made of a non-existing (thing) with a non-existing (thing, would certainly be (a comparision) of the horn of a donkey with the horn of a hare.

ekena tu pramāṇena sarvajño yena kalpyate,
nūnaṃ sa cakṣuṣā sarvān rasādīn pratipadyate.
(p. 38)

That man, by whom with the help of only one *pramāṇa* (=a means of acquiring a correct notion or right perception) an omniscient being is assumed (to be there), indeed perceives all (objects such as) an object of taste (*rasa*) etc. (i.e. an object of smell, touch, and sound) with the eye.

kalpanīyāś ca sarvajñā bhaveyur bahavas tava,
ya eva syād asarvajñaḥ sa sarvajñaṃ na budhyate.
(p. 38)

Moreover, according to you, many omniscient beings should be assumed. (For a man) who is not an omniscient, cannot recognize (somebody) as an omniscient.

ghaṭāyonmīlitaṃ cakṣuḥ paṭaṃ na hi na budhyate,
etad eva prasaktavyaṃ viṣayasyāpi saṃskṛtau.
(p. 40)

The eye, which is opened (to see) a pot, would also certainly see a cloth (near by it. Lit. the eye opened for a pot certainly does not a cloth not know). The same should happen even in (the theory of) purification of an object.

tasmād acalato 'pi syāc calane kartṛtātmanaḥ,
yathaivābhidyamānasya devadattasya bhettṛtā.
(p. 42)

Just as Devadatta becomes an agent of breaking (something, remaining himself) unbroken, (in the same way), therefore the Ātman (the soul), although (he himself) does not move, becomes the agent of moving (his body etc.).

saṃvṛter na tu satyatvaṃ satyabhedaḥ kuto nv ayam,
satyaṃ cet saṃvṛtiḥ keyaṃ mṛṣā cet satyatā katham.
(p. 53)

Falsity cannot be truth indeed. Wherefrom (comes this) difference in the truth? If (it is) a truth, how can the same be a falsity (lit. what is this falsity)? If (it is) a falsity, how (can the same be) a truth? (Here the author attacks the Buddhists who accept the false truth (*saṃvṛti-satyam*) and the real truth (*pāramārthikasatyam*).

sarvavākyamṛṣātve tu dharmoktyaivātmabādhanam,
dharmyuktyāhaṃ yato jātaḥ sā vandhyā jananī mama.
(p. 54)

If all verbal statements are false, (there is), indeed a self-contradiction by mentioning the attribute (of a verbal statement, i.e. falsity). (In the statement):

"My mother, from whom I was born, is a barren woman" (there is a self-contradiction) by mentioning the bearer of attribute (*dharmin*).

ākāśe 'vasthitāḥ śabdāḥ saṃskartuṃ śakyate kathaṃ,
nityatvān mūrtyabhāvāc ca vyomāśritavibhutvavat.
(p. 57)

The word-elements remain in the ether. Moreover, (they), just as all-pervasiveness of the sky, (are) eternal and devoid of form. How it is possible to purify them (with grammar) ?

eko rogo hato yasya yasya vāpahṛtā daśa,
arogitve tayor bhedo na kaś cid api vidyate.
(p. 58)

Whether one disease of a person was removed or ten diseases of some other person were removed, (so far as) diseaselessness (is concerned), there is no difference between them.

na ca śīghrahṛte 'rthe 'sti cirād āgacchato gatiḥ,
aśvair apahṛtaṃ ko hi gardabhaiḥ prāptum icchati.
(p. 61)

(A person), approaching slowly, cannot (have) wish for a quickly removed object. For who would wish to get (back) a thing with the help of donkeys when it was carried away with (the help of) horses ?

paratrāvinayaṃ kurvan pitṛbhyāṃ vāryate sutaḥ,
tayor evāvinītasya ko bhaved vinivārakaḥ.
(p. 63)

A son, behaving rudely towards others, (can) be prevented (from such misbehaviour) by his parents. (Suppose if the same son) misbehaves towards them (i.e. towards his own parents) who could keep check on him ?

loke tu sarvabhāṣābhir arthā vyākaraṇād ṛte,
sidhyanti vyavahāreṇa kāvyādiṣv apy asaṃśayam.
(p. 68)

Meanings (of words) in all languages are certainly established in the world by the usage (even) without grammar. Undoubtedly, (this is the procedure) even in the case of poetical compositions.